OUTRAGEOUS WOMEN OF THE MIDDLE AGES

by Vicki León

John Wiley & Sons, Inc.

New York • Chichester • Weinheim • Brisbane • Singapore • Toronto

Copyright © 1998 by Vicki León
Illustrations copyright © 1998 by Lisa M. Brown
Maps copyright © 1998 by Jessica Wolk-Stanley
Designed by BTD/Robin Bentz and Ann Obringer
Published by John Wiley & Sons, Inc.

The poem on page 114 is from *Women Poets of China*, translated by Ken Rexroth and Chung Ling, © 1982 by New Directions. Reprinted with permission.

This publication is designed to provide accurate and authoritative information in regard to the subject matter covered. It is sold with the understanding that the publisher is not engaged in rendering professional services. If professional advice or other expert assistance is required, the services of a competent professional person should be sought.

LIBRARY OF CONGRESS CATALOGING-IN-PUBLICATION DATA
León, Vicki
      Outrageous women of the Middle Ages / Vicki León.
         p.   cm. -- (Outrageous women series)
      Includes index.
      Summary: Biographies of some outspoken and influential women who
lived in Europe, Africa, and the Far East during the Middle Ages.
      ISBN 0-471-17004-6 (pbk. : alk. paper)
      1. Women--Biography--Juvenile literature. 2. Biography--Middle
Ages, 500-1500--Juvenile literature. 3. Women--History--Juvenile
literature. 4. Civilization, Medieval--Juvenile literature.
      [1. Women--History--500-1500. 2. Women--Biography.] I. Title.
II. Series
      CT3220.L46   1998
      920.72'09'02--dc21   97-30307

Printed in the United States of America

C O N T E N T S

The next time you pick up a book about the Middle Ages, try a little experiment I've been doing for years. Go to the index at the back and run your finger down the names. Find many women's names? If you ran across more than a saint and a queen or two, you're lucky. No wonder that girls and women alike feel left out when it comes to the past. Instead of fearless fore-mothers and daring daughters, our history books tend to give us monotonous lists of wars and dates, male rulers and rogues.

This doesn't mean that women of the Middle Ages, also called the Medieval Era, sat around on their tuffets, waiting for knights in shining armor. Women back then did plenty. As I discovered in my research, women everywhere were the glue of their societies, although they got little credit. In addition to birthing babies, doing the cooking, making everyone's clothes, and other standard womanly pursuits, these tough cookies were often on their own, sometimes for years. While their menfolk were away fighting wars, going on crusades, or traveling on business, women had to run the grand estates and the tiny farms. They had to pay the taxes and handle legal matters. They had to support their families—and sometimes defend their homes, villages, and castles.

We often hear the Middle Ages called the "dark ages," an era when progress stopped and learning was lost. It's true that the years from 500 to 1350 were filled with worldwide plagues, crop failures, political failures, and famine. But that doesn't mean that civilization just stood still.

In many ways, these eight centuries were a period of great movement and change. Vikings from Scandinavia and roaming tribes from Asia and elsewhere trotted the globe, exploring and raiding. These newcomers made life difficult (sometimes impossible) for those already on the scene—which, in turn, caused some men and women to seek a new life elsewhere.

By the year 500, the Roman Empire had faded but its eastern half, called the Byzantine Empire, remained strong. In it, women such as the historian Anna Comnena pursued their goals. Anna's home city of Constantinople, capital of the Byzantine Empire, was a huge and luxurious city. In contrast, most Europeans lived in small villages or walled cities belonging to a lord or lady. Famous queens such as Eleanor of Aquitaine and lesser nobility such as Countess Mahaut of Artois spent much of their time as traveling landladies, visiting their domains.

On the other side of the world in Asia, the largely peaceful and creative centuries from 600 to 1200 saw many women in positions of honor and importance. Murasaki Shikibu, the world's first novelist, had a strong following in Japan. Li Ch'ing-chao, the most important female poet ever to write a love lyric in China, achieved equal fame. The Silla kingdom in southern Korea could have been called a "queendom." It had three female rulers, as well as other women who are now thought to have co-ruled with their kingly husbands.

In Europe, religion and everyday life were one. Many women found fulfillment (and a way to a good education) by becoming nuns, one of the few socially acceptable alternatives to marriage. Christian leaders like Clare of Assisi and Hildegard of Bingen became role models. Their dedication, and their growing celebrity, helped build enthusiasm for the movement called the Crusades. For two centuries, these Christian wars over the Holy Land influenced societies in Europe and the Middle East. Hundreds of thousands of men took part, traveling for years at a time. Although everyone called them "holy wars," the Crusades butchered many innocent people. Jews were a special target. Thousands of Jews killed by the crusaders are still remembered in the Yom Kippur liturgy each year.

Surprisingly, thousands of women and children took part in the Crusades, too. Most took a vow as pilgrims (people who traveled to a religious shrine), not as soldiers.

Religion played a huge role in life elsewhere, too. A new spirituality called Buddhism spread from India to China, Japan, and other lands of the Far East. Empresses like Koken and Komyo built temples and put up huge works of art to express their devotion. In the Middle East, a religion called Islam blossomed in Arabia and spread across North Africa. At its heart were a number of active women—including Khadija, the first wife (and the first disciple) of Mohammed the Prophet.

Identifying and choosing the women in this book wasn't hard. Finding out the truth about them was. At times, these bold women went against the grain, outraging their families and their societies, upsetting the status quo. Historians of their day (and later ones, too) often disapproved of their actions. Until recent centuries, there were no libel laws or rules about truth in journalism, so historians could write about women in a negative way, or invent tales. Chroniclers also felt free to use famous or notorious women as examples of the awful things that could happen if a woman rose to power!

These life stories aren't as complete as we'd like them to be. You may not learn the things you'd most like to know: the color of a woman's eyes and hair, her favorite foods, what she laughed at, what she detested, and what she dreamed of doing. Earlier writers didn't feel that such details about a person were important. Only rarely was a medieval woman ever depicted as an individual in a painting, or her ordinary speech quoted accurately in writing by a person who actually knew her.

Fortunately, sources still exist that allow us to gather fuller information about women of the past. In cities all over Europe, for instance, there are church documents, court records, and city archives that have been gathering dust since they were written. A new generation of committed scholars and historians (many of them women) are busy delving into these rich, often untapped records of medieval times to trace women's lives.

We also have the help of archaeology to flesh out the half-hidden histories of women, a source that adds to our knowledge daily. Take the case of Queen Sonduk of Korea, who is profiled in this book. After archaeologists began to dig at the royal burial mounds in Kyong-ju, they discovered that women had far more political importance in Silla (one of the three kingdoms in medieval Korea) than had been thought. Their discoveries of gold jewelry, royal crowns, and other artifacts belonging to royalty like Sonduk have overturned our old ideas about women's roles in this society.

Besides the treasures of Korean queens, numerous other artifacts created by medieval women have survived to our day. As you read on, you'll learn about books, poems, music, artwork, religious artifacts—even monuments and buildings left by our outrageous achievers. Like the bits of colored glass that make the stained-glass windows of medieval cathedrals so beautiful, these pieces of evidence,

HIGH-RISE HEADGEAR WAS HIP IN MEDIEVAL KOREA.

put together, form a picture glowing with life. They show us the shimmering qualities that these fifteen women, drawn from cultures around the globe, had in common.

Part One

BRITISH ISLES, FRANCE, AND SCANDINAVIA

VIKING RAIDERS

Other peoples feared the raids of the Vikings, and with good reason. In their fast, highly seaworthy ships with pointed prows and rectangular sails of red wool, the Vikings could swoop down on a settlement with no warning. Viking boys and girls like Aud grew up on the water. They learned from their elders how to navigate by reading the subtle signs of the sea, the clouds, and the stars.

CHAPTER 1

Aud the Deep-Minded

T he Vikings are coming!" For nearly three hundred years (roughly 780 to 1070), that phrase struck fear into hearts from Ireland to Russia. But these Scandinavian sea raiders, also known as Norsemen, weren't merely male warriors out for blood and booty. There were just as many female Vikings—like the surprising Aud Djupaudga, also known as Unn.

Aud grew up in a big Viking family from Romsdale, Norway, the second daughter of Yngvid and a great chieftain called Ketil Flatnose. Tall and muscular even as a child, Aud shot up like a weed.

Aud was full grown but still unmarried when her family had to leave Norway. An aggressive king called Harald Fairhair wanted to rule it all. "Become my vassals or lose your freedom!" he said to chieftains like Ketil. Always independent, Ketil and the others refused.

Aud's two older brothers decided to go to Iceland, a new country far to the west. But her father said, "I'm too old to settle a new land. We'll go to the Southern Islands." So Aud, her parents, and her other siblings settled in the Hebrides, a group of starkly beautiful islands sprinkled along Scotland's western coast.

During the long periods when her father was away, trading for fur pelts or attacking settlements to capture gold or slaves, Aud and her mother became attracted to the Christian way of life practiced by the Celtic people on the Hebrides. Instead of worshipping the Viking gods and goddesses, mother and daughter embraced the Christian faith—and converted the rest of the family. Educated at

EVERYDAY RELIGION

Although Aud and her family became Christians, many Vikings continued to honor the old Scandinavian way of worship for centuries. Most Viking holy places were in the open air, where deities such as Thor the sky god, Odin the war god, and Freya the goddess of love were worshipped. People often wore religious amulets, such as the hammer of Thor. Aud herself may have been buried with a Christian cross and a Viking amulet for tradition's sake. Viking religion still influences our lives in surprising ways—we call the days of the week Wednesday, Thursday, and Friday in honor of the gods Woden and Thor and the goddess Freya.

home by her mother, Aud took her studies of theology and philosophy seriously, becoming something of a wise woman and teacher. The Vikings, who were as fond of nicknames as they were of drinking strong mead wine, started calling her Aud the Deep-Minded.

We don't know if Aud had a flat nose like her father, but she did inherit the Viking itchy foot and independence of spirit. After marrying a Viking chieftain named Olaf the White, she left her home in the Hebrides for Ireland. Olaf called himself king of

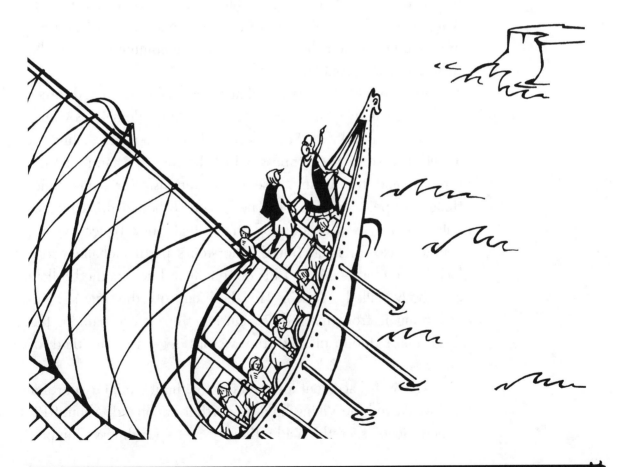

Ireland; he dominated the emerald isle from his raid headquarters at the seaport town of Dublin, which he founded.

Aud soon had a son called Thorstein the Red. But Aud's marriage didn't last. Either she divorced Olaf, or he died in battle. The records aren't clear about what happened to her next—she may have returned to the Hebrides, gone to Scotland, or both. Eventually, she became a woman of high standing in the Viking community on the Hebrides.

When her son Thorstein grew up, he turned into an able fighter like his father and grandfather. He married and had six daughters and several sons. Aud found that she liked being a grandmother. When she wasn't busy as a community leader, she fussed over her grandkids.

Around 900, Thorstein and another Viking combined forces against the native Scots, carving out a huge domain covering the northern half of Scotland. Aud and her grandchildren joined Thorstein at Caithness, which became the family home, fortress, and the Viking base of operations. For some time, things ran peacefully in Aud's new Scottish homeland. Unfortunately, peace was a state of affairs that your typical Viking couldn't take for long. Bored, Thorstein's partner challenged a local to combat and killed his opponent (a buck-toothed fellow everybody called "Tusk"). He then cut off the man's head and hung it from his saddle. During the victory parade, the dead man's tooth pierced the victor's leg—and he died of infection.

This weird accident left Aud's son without a military partner and weakened the Viking hold on northern Scotland. About 915, armed Scots secretly made their way to Caithness, jumped

Thorstein, and killed him. When Aud got word of her son's death, she knew that she had to act.

She gave urgent orders to build a ship in the hidden depths of a forest near the sea. When it was finished, the energetic grandmother loaded the vessel with food supplies and valuables from silver to amber. Then she hurried every surviving member of her family and clan on board: from grandchildren and relatives to nobles, loyal followers, and family slaves.

Setting sail to the north, Aud's first stop was the Orkney Islands. The earl who ruled them was friendly; she and her clan could have made a home there. But the Orkneys seemed too cramped. Since it never hurt to have a fall-back, Aud shrewdly arranged for her granddaughter Groa to marry the earl.

Again Aud lifted sail, heading northwest. Finally, she sighted the bare volcanic cliffs of the islands called the Faroes, famous mainly for their year-round rains. Aud found more friendly faces, but she still hankered to go on.

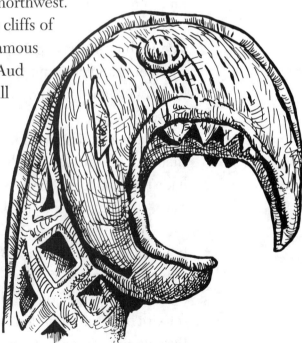

"Tell me more of the place they call Snowland or Iceland," she asked others around the evening fire in the hearth. "My brothers went there long ago." She heard conflicting tales. "A huge land, difficult to sail to, but worthy," some said. "A dangerous place belching fire," declared others.

Aud decided to take the plunge. Before setting off, she made a firm political ally on the Faroes by marrying Olof, another grand-daughter, to a man who owned much land there.

Aud needed all the skills she could summon for this next voyage. Her ship, most likely a *knorr* built of oak and pine and affectionately called "goat of the sea" by the Vikings, was as sturdy as they came. Nevertheless, she'd be sailing through nearly three hundred miles of open ocean, far from any land. A big storm or a small miscalculation, and they'd be doomed.

Watching the bronze flag of her ship's wind vane like a hawk, Aud used the prevailing winds to sail north. Finally she and the crew saw the petrel birds the Faroe Islanders had told them about.

They'd made it to Iceland! The deep fjords and snowy mountains of Iceland's coast reminded Aud of Norway. Beneath the waters, however, reefs like sharks' teeth lay hidden. While looking for safe harbor, Aud's ship hit a reef and sank. Despite the wild surf she, her grandkids, and the rest of her group made it to shore—along with most of the goods and valuables they'd brought on board.

Bedraggled and cold, Aud and twenty of her people found their way to the sod farmhouse of her brother Helgi, whom she hadn't seen for over 30 years. Instead of hugs and hospitality, Helgi said, "I have room for only half of you."

Aud must have been furious. Fuming, she headed for the home of her other brother Bjorn. Before she even reached Bjorn's homestead, he and his family came to greet them. Aud and the others got a warm welcome at his house; Bjorn had no wish to quarrel with his strong-minded sister! He invited them to stay with him through the winter, fast approaching.

In the spring, Aud set off to find her own spot to settle in. She sailed along the western coast of Iceland, exploring the river valleys now lush with flowers and green grass, stopping at each headland she fancied.

Whenever Aud found a promising site for settlement, she went ashore and lit a ritual bonfire, the traditional Viking way of saying "I claim this land." To honor her faith, she also set up Christian crosses, it was said. Aud couldn't stop shopping, either. She lit bonfires along over 180 square miles of land, most of which she gave away to her people, including her slaves.

At last, Aud sailed into a particularly deep fjord, and made her way into its innermost bay. When she went ashore to explore it, she made a marvelous discovery. The pillars from her old home, lost in the shipwreck, lay washed up on the shore.

MAKE YOUR HOME WHERE THE PILLAR LANDS

Vikings moved a lot. One thing that went from place to place with them were their high-seat pillars. These two carved pieces of wood sat on either side of the seat of honor in each Viking home. They brought the household good luck. Among the Norwegian Vikings in particular, it was a tradition to put them on board ship when you set out to settle a new place. Once you caught sight of land, you pushed the pillars overboard. Then you would build your new home at the spot where they washed ashore. If you were a Viking, you couldn't be in a hurry about starting your new home: sometimes it took several years before the good luck charms washed up!

"This will be where my new house and farm will stand!" proclaimed Aud. She named it Hvamm; it's been called that ever since by the Icelanders.

Although her step was still brisk, and her arms strong, Aud was getting up in years. She went to bed early, and rarely rose before noon. Touchy about her health, Aud crabbed at people who asked after it. By now, she had gotten all of her grandchildren settled and happily married except one. When Olaf, her youngest grandson, became a man, Aud left her comfortable sod home at Hvamm and set out to choose a wife for him. (As the family matriarch, she had that privilege.) That autumn, she put on the greatest wedding feast Iceland had yet seen, inviting pioneer families and relatives from many miles away to attend.

When all had gathered for the festivities, Aud the Deep-Minded greeted the guests and gave a little speech. "Thank you for coming—I want you to witness that my home, and everything that

ICELANDIC WOMEN: THE BUM'S RUSH IN THE LAND RUSH

Early explorers and settlers like Aud, who nabbed 180 square miles of Iceland, had no limits on the land they could claim. Later settlers had to abide by more stringent rules. For instance, it became the law that a man could claim all the land he was able to walk around in a single day while carrying a torch. Women had a separate—but not very equal—law: a woman could claim all the land she could walk around in one day. The catch was, she had to lead a two-year-old cow while walking!

goes with it, I now give to my grandson Olaf Feilan and his new wife Alfdis." Everyone applauded.

Aud then made sure that there was plenty of boiled meat and other feast dishes on hand. She checked to see that the ale and the mead were flowing freely. Satisfied, she said, "Enjoy yourselves!" and marched off to bed, leaving the new couple and the others to celebrate the night away.

The next day, Olaf went looking for his grandmother. Going into her bedroom, he found her lifeless body propped against her pillows, sitting up in bed like a proud Viking matriarch.

Olaf went to tell the others the sad news. "What dignity she had, to her dying day!" they said. Now the wedding feast became a funeral feast, too. On the last day of the feast, they placed Aud's body in a small Viking ship and surrounded it with treasure. She was buried in the ground below the high-water mark of the tides, where the waters of the Atlantic could moisten her grave with salt tears twice a day.

CHAPTER 2

Matilda of England

Medieval England was full of Matildas with blue blood. But none had a more proud pedigree than the dark-haired baby girl born in February of 1102. On her mother Matilda's side, she counted 14 kings. On her father King Henry I's side, three generations had sat on England's throne.

It was her mother, however, who taught Matilda how to survive in a rough, tough man's world. Matilda's mother had been raised in a nunnery, where a good slapping and horrible scolding were part of the education. Remembering her "school of hard knocks," this mother made sure that young Matilda learned her ABCs at home. When the little girl wanted to learn embroidery, her mother said, "It's better that you learn to train others to embroider well, my child." With this and other lessons, Queen Matilda, lovingly called "Good Queen Mold" by her English subjects, prepared her daughter for the royal duties that lay ahead.

At the tender age of seven, Princess Matilda found out about duty number one. "You're going to be married to the emperor of the Holy Roman Empire," her parents announced. Right after that, she made her first official appearance, witnessing a royal charter. Holding a pen, Matilda made a careful cross next to the line that said: *sponsa regis Romanorum* or "the betrothed wife of the King of the Romans."

In 1110, the little princess traveled across the rough gray seas of the English Channel to the imposing city of Liège, France. The only familiar thing about her fiancé was his name: he was also a Henry! When Matilda met her 24-year-old husband-to-be for the first time, she was surrounded by a sea of attendants and a pack train of animals carrying hundreds of sacks loaded with her dowry of ten thousand pieces of silver. The two set off for an official tour of her new land.

Archive Photos, ID#10112215. Used with permission.

LOTS OF SILVER, NO TOASTERS FOR THIS CHILD BRIDE.

THE HOLY ROMAN EMPIRE

Covering most of present-day Germany, and at times parts of Italy and France, the Holy Roman Empire was basically a loose coalition of European states. The first and most famous emperor was Charlemagne, whose talent at winning territories and governing was recognized by Pope Leo III. In the year 800 the pope crowned him emperor, and the newly invented Holy Roman Empire was off and rolling. Few of its later emperors had Charlemagne's talent; still, this clever way of linking the interests of the Catholic Church to royal power lasted for a thousand years.

On July 25 of that year, young Matilda was crowned Empress of the Holy Roman Empire. Her marriage to Henry, however, didn't take place until four years later, just before her twelfth birthday. Countless nobles attended the wedding. Matilda and Henry got so many bridal gifts that the helpers lost count!

By now, Matilda had received more schooling in German, French, and the correct behavior for an empress. In her new home, women did more of the work of government than in England; the young empress learned to preside over courts and other official duties. Matilda often got to travel with her husband on royal business. Their lands, running from what we'd call Germany in the north to Rome in the south, were hard to reach and even harder to manage. Their vassals or lords were quick to pledge loyalty—but very slow to pay taxes. Henry was always at them, asking for the money he needed to run the Holy Roman Empire.

In 1120, Matilda got the tragic news that her own mother, Good Queen Mold, had died. A bare year later, she got another shock: a new stepmother. Her father, now in his fifties, had mar-

THE MERCY TOUCH

In times of old, it became traditional for people in trouble, knights in disgrace, and families wanting justice for a wrong to petition their queen or empress for help. These petitions were called intercessions or grants. If the plea had merit, the queen would take the petition to the king or emperor. Matilda was a very generous and competent ruler in this respect. Over the years, Matilda won so many mercies, pardons, and favors from Emperor Henry on behalf of others that she gained the nickname "the good Matilda."

ried an 18-year-old, a French count's daughter. Her name was Adeliza Louvein, but everyone called her "the fair maid of Brabant" for her beauty and gentle nature.

Even at a distance, Matilda was prepared to dislike Adeliza. In 1125, however, a new sadness captured all her attention. Her own husband, the Emperor of the Holy Roman Empire, died. In her grief, Matilda found herself coolly treated—possibly because she and Henry had no children. "It would be best if you got yourself into a religious order," those in power around her said, "or maybe we could try to find a suitable new husband for you."

Indignant, Matilda did neither. She returned to England, to her father's household. The former empress traveled light, bringing little more than her magnificent set of jewels, a silver box said to contain the egg of a griffin (a mythical beast), and a holy relic that was believed to be the hand of Saint James.

THE RELIGIOUS CRAZE OF RELICS

In 1110, during her coronation ceremony in a German chapel on the Feast of St. James, Matilda first saw one of the holiest relics in Europe—the hand of Saint James. It may have impressed her more than her crown. When she left the Holy Roman Empire as a new widow, she took the relic with her. The hand was just one of hundreds—perhaps thousands—of holy relics highly admired in medieval times. Relics were bones or objects thought to belong to saints, or such things as pieces of the cross on which Christ was crucified. The devout considered them as cures, magical amulets, and objects of worship. Many were not genuine, of course. In the churches throughout Europe, there were said to be enough "pieces of the True Cross" to build a good-sized boat!

Her father was very glad to see her. He looked old and weary. His sons had died. His new wife still hadn't gotten pregnant, after four years. Matilda was his one legitimate child. "My hopes for leaving this land to my descendants rest with you," he said.

Matilda was mightily pleased; now all she faced was the ordeal of meeting her father's new wife. She braced herself to greet Adeliza. A proud brunette, Matilda towered over her tiny blonde stepmother. Adeliza had an easy-going personality, the complete opposite of Matilda's stubborn, often haughty ways. The only thing they had in common was age: they were both in their early twenties. To everyone's surprise, stepdaughter and stepmother became fast friends.

Matilda's father soon pushed her to remarry. "I have the perfect candidate," he said. It was bad enough when Matilda learned that his "perfect" man was a 16-year-old named Geoffrey from Anjou, France. The part that really upset her was the boy's status. "Geoffrey's not even a count!" she huffed. "I'll make him one!" said Henry.

Father and daughter fought endlessly. Stepmother Adeliza acted as a buffer zone, letting Matilda stay in her quarters and trying to reconcile the two. Finally Matilda gave in. Much as she hated it sometimes, she believed that leaders had duties—which in her case included producing an heir to the throne.

She married Geoffrey and moved to Anjou about 1128; within a year, their marriage was on the rocks. Out of patience with her teen husband, Matilda left him three separate times and returned to England. In a couple of years, however, Geoffrey seemed to have matured. He sent "please come back" messages, and promised to honor Matilda as she deserved. Meanwhile, at Henry's request, many of the English nobles had given their oath of loyalty to Matilda. The old king knew that his daughter would need their full support to be proclaimed queen after he died.

In 1131, therefore, Matilda went back to France. Soon she and Geoffrey had a baby on the way. To everyone's utter delight, it was a boy! Matilda said, "We'll name him (no surprise) Henry." Little Henry (who would someday be Henry the Second, the first Plantagenet king of England) had flaming red hair and a temper to match; a year later, he got a brother named Geoffrey.

The fond English grandfather had a few short years to enjoy his grandsons before dying in France in December 1135. The family was still mourning when Matilda's first cousin Stephen roared over to England, stormed London, and got himself acclaimed as king. Matilda was in shock. The earlier pledges to her by the English nobles had been lies!

"I need to build a bigger power base to win this throne," she said. Bulky and pregnant with her third child, Matilda got on her horse. In the bitter cold, she and husband Geoffrey made the rounds of the border castles of Normandy. The castles were her dowry; their lords owed her allegiance. One by one, she slowly received their pledges of support.

In 1139, she made her move. Matilda crossed the English Channel and headed for Arundel Castle. Its knightly owner supported her cousin Stephen; however, the noble lady of the castle was Adeliza, now remarried but still Matilda's dear friend. Once again Adeliza gave Matilda safe haven, the first step toward her goal.

Despite Adeliza's continued help, Matilda and her forces fought Stephen for fifteen months. Finally, she took him prisoner.

Now in chains, Stephen still had a secret weapon: his own clever queen—whose name was *also* Matilda.

The two Matildas struggled, each trying to win over the majority of English vassals. Just when our Matilda thought she had the crown in her pocket, with the coronation all arranged, she made a bad move. Londoners asked her for tax relief; instead of relief, she demanded more money. The city folk turned against her. When she showed up for her coronation, they chased her out

of London. While Matilda and company were beating a retreat to Oxford, the rascally Londoners gobbled up the banquet laid for the ceremony!

By 1142, Matilda realized she'd never be accepted as queen of England. But she kept on trying for Henry, her young son's sake. If she couldn't rule, then Henry would. He must! When he turned 14, the boy tried to help his mom by bringing a band of knights from France. After failing to storm two castles, the teen found out that fighting wasn't as easy as it looked. Even more embarrassing, he had to ask his mom for money in order to pay his men.

Ultimately, Matilda did reach her goal. She lived to see her son Henry the Second crowned King of England, the first of the famous Plantagenet kings. (The Plantagenets were the Kennedys of their day—a 200-year dynasty of vital and well-loved monarchs.) She saw eight grandchildren from Henry and her daughter-in-law, Eleanor of Aquitaine. And on her tombstone, they placed the legend: "Great by birth, greater by marriage, greatest in her offspring." Good Queen Mold would have been proud.

CHAPTER 3

Eleanor of Aquitaine

(ABOUT 1122–1204)

Eleanor of Aquitaine, the most celebrated queen of the Middle Ages, caused a stir wherever she went. And that was quite a distance: a royal with more business miles than many a frequent flyer, she traveled from the lush lands of southern France to the cool woods of England to the burning stretches of North Africa and the Middle East. She hit almost every great city of the day, and a lot of terrain in between. (Eleanor did it the hard way, too: on horseback or by boat.)

Her eventful eighty-two years began with her birth in Aquitaine, "land of waters," the oak-forested river valleys of what is now central and southern France. For three generations, dukes named William (including Eleanor's own father) had ruled these vineyards, orchards, and villages from the Loire River to the Pyrenees Mountains. Now there were no more Williams to inherit; she was the last of her line.

"Gracious, lovely, a wind from paradise," the musicians and

poets at the court in Poitiers, the capital city of Aquitaine, called her in song and verse. Female beauty in her day meant long shiny hair, a straight nose, and wide-set eyes. Eleanor surpassed that ideal; she had dark hair and eyes, and the complexion of an Irish rose. She had more than good looks, too—she was robustly alive, an imaginative girl, poised and full of fun, a lover of music and song like her grandfather William of Poitou, who'd composed and sung the first troubadour lyrics about romantic passion.

But Eleanor's early life was not all happy. She lost her mother Aenor when she was eight; her father was constantly involved in wars and political battles. Eleanor's grandmother and her ladies-in-waiting found the child quite a handful. Defiant and restless, self-centered and tomboyish, Eleanor sat still only long enough to get a first-class education. She learned several languages and reading was her special joy—above all, she loved to read and sing the poetry of the troubadours.

By the time they were in their teens, Eleanor and her sister Petronilla had the young men of the court at their feet. Batting their charcoal-lined eyes, giggling and flirting, the girls called the shots. Their favorite pastime? Doing uncanny imitations of the pompous dignitaries visiting Aquitaine.

In 1137, their father went on a pilgrimage to seek a step-mother for his daughters; instead, he fell deathly ill. Worried because his only heir was young and female, Eleanor's father put his trust in the hands of the French King Louis the Sixth, more often called "Louis the Fat." Before he died, he sent a message to the king: "Please keep Eleanor and her inheritance safe, and find her a suitable husband to rule over Aquitaine."

Louis the Fat was delighted. He had a not-so-secret passion

WOMEN IN THE MUSICAL SPOTLIGHT— FEMALE TROUBADOURS

Troubadours were singers and poets who composed in the popular language of the south of France, called *langue d'oc.* They became hugely popular in the twelfth and thirteenth centuries. Eleanor's grandfather started the troubadour trend; Eleanor was a huge fan and a music lover who paid for many a musician at her court in France, and later in England.

Troubadouring wasn't just for guys, either—women got into the musical act, both as performers and as composers. The lyrics written by the female troubadours were a bit like our country and western songs—all about relationships and the rocky road to love. (The men tended to write about idealized love.) Some twenty female troubadours have been identified so far.

to annex Aquitaine. He could also make good on the duke's last request: conveniently at hand was his sixteen-year-old son and heir, Louis the Seventh, called "the Young." By June, he'd ripped Louis away from the religious devotions he was crazy about, and sent the pale blond boy south, escorted by five hundred men.

Eleanor met her new groom in mid-July. He was shy, tall, and thin, with a weak mouth, more pretty than handsome. The wedding party was extravagant in the Aquitaine style. After days of feasting on swan and lobster, candied fruits and tarts, washed down with quantities of good red wine, and enlivened with the sounds of flutes, lutes, and troubadour song, young Louis could barely see straight. Instead of a honeymoon, the newlyweds traveled around Aquitaine in the August heat, meeting people and receiving their homage.

Not everyone was pleased about Eleanor's marriage; in fact, one angry vassal (a noble who owed allegiance to a lord or lady) kidnapped two of the new groom's knights. Before he knew it, Louis found himself in hand-to-hand combat. To end the fracas, he and his men killed the rebels. That derring-do won Eleanor's respect: maybe this mild little lamb she'd married was a man after all!

That same week in August, the old king died of fever, so obese he couldn't even be carried into the chapel. Eleanor and Louis hurried to Paris; she was now declared Queen of France and her young husband, King Louis the Seventh. Paris was a shock to Eleanor—a dirty, uncivilized place. Even the Cité Palace where she lived was a mess! Once she'd made her new home more comfortable, she tried to help Louis with affairs of state. Heaven knows he could have used it; weak and young, inexperienced in life and leadership, more a monk than a king, Louis also had a tendency to cry easily. These traits didn't endear him to Eleanor. She wasn't especially pious, and she never cried.

But Eleanor's efforts to help met with little success. Although in times past, French queens had made policy and helped their husbands run things, this time the throne had a string attached to it—a string named Abbot Suger, key political adviser to the old king. Suger loved young Louis, whom he found delightfully easy to manipulate. Eleanor and Suger were on opposite sides, and the Abbot usually won out.

With these frustrations, it's easy to see why, after ten years of marriage and two baby girls (instead of the all-important male heir), Eleanor was even more eager than Louis to take part in the great adventure of her times: the Second Crusade. For a year prior to setting out, she was a blur of motion: frantically collecting money to fund the operation, recruiting soldiers—even convincing a group of noblewomen to accompany her on this holy quest to Jerusalem.

On a bright blue day in June 1147, they set out, over 100,000 strong. Eleanor, wearing cherry-red boots and a white tunic with the red cross of the crusader on her chest, galloped at the head of her flamboyant group of high-society Amazons, mounted on white horses. Brandishing a sword, she urged even more people to take the cross. Thanks to Eleanor, there were more knights from Aquitaine on the crusade than from any other place.

With an operation this big, many things could go wrong. And they did. The biggest problem was lack of leadership; he might have been holy, but Louis was a flop at command. He dawdled; he dithered; he failed to keep parts of the crusading army from

At the end of the eleventh century, the notion of a Christian holy war against the Seljuk Turks who held the Holy Land found great acceptance. The Crusades were a community goal—and a way to wash away your own personal sins. They were viewed as an adventure for those who craved excitement, and a socially admired way to release aggressions—even kill others (as long as the victims weren't Christians!) and be praised for it. One Crusade spawned another. There were eight "great" Crusades, two ill-fated Children's Crusades (pictured here), and countless smaller, regional ones. Records on the Children's Crusades are scanty; it's thought that thousands of boys (and a few girls) from France and Germany took part. Most were sold as slaves, died of sickness, or otherwise vanished even before they left the European continent.

Only briefly did any of the Crusades manage to achieve their goal of capturing Jerusalem. In terms of lives lost, the Crusades killed far more crusaders, pilgrims, hangers-on, and innocent bystanders than they ever did "infidels." Nevertheless, this massive, centuries-long movement of people increased trade between the Middle East and Europe, introduced new products (pottery hand grenades, for instance), and as an unintended bonus, gave women minding the castles and cottages at home a chance to use their abilities more fully.

fighting and killing one another; when supplies ran out, he couldn't get locals to provide them. Then the *real* troubles began: ambushes, bloody massacres by the Turks, near starvation, a flash flood in their campsite, a ghastly march through the mountains in a winter storm, plague in the camp. By the time Eleanor had suffered through a three-week storm-tossed voyage from Turkey to her uncle's stronghold city of Antioch in Syria, she was hardly speaking to her husband. And they were still at least two months away from Jerusalem!

Eleanor had had it. She told Louis that she wanted to stay in Antioch and get a divorce, but Louis dragged her away by force and on to Jerusalem. The queen refused to reconcile with him. Later, with the pathetic remnants of their crusader troops, the two visited the pope in Rome. His efforts at mending the marriage didn't work, either. They took separate ships back to France. There Eleanor set about the slow process of getting a divorce and the important task of getting her own lands of Aquitaine back. Louis, meanwhile, got involved in a small war with two of the Plantagenet clan, which by 1151 he had lost.

That August in Paris was one of the hottest anyone could remember. The temperature went up a few more degrees when Geoffrey of Anjou and his son, Henry, arrived to negotiate a settlement. A thunderbolt struck Eleanor when she saw Henry. His short red hair, his bristling energy, and his outdoor ways attracted her instantly. He was eighteen; in Eleanor, he saw a woman of twenty-nine at her glorious peak. Within months, they were wed.

Things continued to move fast. In 1154, Eleanor's new husband, thanks to some bold military moves and a lot of uncanny good luck, went from being a mere duke of Normandy to being crowned King Henry the Second of England. Eleanor became England's new queen. Having suffered through Paris winters at one chilly palace, Eleanor knew what to bring to her new land. This time, along with her trousseau of forty-two embroidered gowns, she packed ten warm undershirts!

As they toured the island in royal procession, the English public quickly nicknamed the ruddy king and his slender, proud wife "the Lion and the Eagle." This time as queen, Eleanor had work responsibilities and financial independence. Henry, whose favorite activity was conquering other lands, was gone often. Eleanor ran the government in his absence, even though she was

pregnant eight times and raised three daughters and five sons. In a few years, she'd proved herself quite capable of replacing her husband; in fact, she was happiest when left to her own devices.

She introduced the French wine industry into England, building her own docks, called Queenhithe, where her ships from Aquitaine tied up. From experience, she'd learned that control of her own money gave her power. Besides her lands in France, she introduced her own system of money collection in England, called "the Queen's gold." (This special tax was unique: No queen before or after raised her own money.)

Henry and Eleanor's lives gradually took separate directions. But no matter which war Henry was fighting, they always spent Christmas together as a special time in one of their homes. But after 1164, for two Yuletides in a row, he didn't show up. Eleanor spent two Christmases alone—each time with a new baby. Gradually Henry also took away her mental stimulus—her work. These actions hurt her deeply; in spite of his black rages and difficult ways, she loved Henry.

As her five boys grew into men, they took sides, mainly against their father. Eleanor's special pets, Richard and Geoffrey, eventually went to war against their father in 1173. Eleanor not only cheered them on—she provided military help from the Aquitaine, whose people remained her subjects, not Henry's. Unfortunately, King Henry beat the boys. Instead of punishing them, he threw Eleanor into prison! For 15 years, she was under house arrest in one drafty castle after another—and only allowed a family visit at Christmas-time.

How she kept sane, we'll never know. But Eleanor didn't let this cruelty break her spirit or body. In 1189, when King Henry died, she bounced back into action. She was sixty-seven years old. After her oldest son, Richard the Lion-Hearted, now king of England, left on the Third Crusade, Eleanor stepped up as regent of the land. Her son Richard was a scrapper and a good-looking redhead over six feet tall (a giant by medieval standards), but he didn't have his dad's talent for military leadership. He lost nearly all of his Crusaders; then he got kidnapped for ransom on his way home. No one wanted to cough up the money—so Eleanor had to get into the act. The pope wouldn't help, even when she threatened him. Finally she paid the huge ransom of 150,000 gold marks herself.

Throughout their entire lives, her boys kept getting into trouble. When Eleanor reached her eighties, they still ran to her for military help. One grandson even tried to take her beloved Aquitaine from her by force! (He didn't succeed.)

Eleanor had better luck running her daughters' lives. Ignoring whatever their personal feelings may have been, she married

MULTIGENERATIONAL POWER WOMEN

When her granddaughter Blanche was eleven, Eleanor's keen eye saw something special. "Here is the maiden who shall be the wife of the king of France," she thought. Even though Eleanor was nearly eighty, she personally escorted her grandchild from Palencia, Spain, to the court of King Louis the Eighth, where Blanche lived until she and the young heir were wed. A strong leader in the manner of her grandmother, Blanche twice ruled France, once for her husband and once for her son. An advocate of health care, she founded a school for surgeons. She also opened many hospitals, and one of them, the Royaumont hospital, is still standing near Paris.

**A BOOKWORM
IN LIFE—AND
BEYOND?**

Granger Collection, #644.33. Used with permission.

them to kings and dukes, building a dynasty throughout Europe. A winner to the last, she retired to Fontevrault, a French convent on a silvery river in her beloved Aquitaine. On her tomb, Eleanor is shown with a faint smile, reading a small book. Perhaps she is savoring one of the passionate poems written about her: the hot-blooded girl in a million, who squeezed and savored every bit of juice from life, both the bitter and the sweet.

Mahaut,
Countess of Artois

(AROUND 1275-1329)

Fond of chess, travel, music, and limited edition books, this glamorous French noblewoman with modern-sounding interests led a remarkable life. She spared no expense on books. One of Mahaut's favorite reads was the *Book of the Great Cham*—the exciting tale of the travels of a certain Marco Polo, who had just returned from an exotic place called China.

Mahaut herself was much more than an armchair traveler. She loved to take journeys around France, and frequently did so. The king of France called her "cousin," but she wasn't as wealthy or as important as a queen. Still, her trips sound pretty luxurious to our ears. Forty servants and sixty horses accompanied her carriage, which was decorated with silver rosettes and midnight blue velvet. (When Mahaut got older, she upgraded to an even more comfy scarlet coach with a silk-covered mattress!) You can't blame her for not wanting to ride horseback all the time: her journeys were often long, the roads poor, and the weather bad.

The countess didn't believe in traveling light. In fact, she brought everything, *including* the kitchen sink: perfume, carving knives, special dainties to eat, and a silver basin for washing milady's hair. Her best books, hand-lettered special editions, hand-painted in gold, traveled in large leather bags; her most prized tapestries and cushions filled the tent she sometimes used for overnight stays.

This cultured woman adored music. She often brought bands of minstrels to the parties and feasts she threw at her homes in the

French cities of Paris, Arras, and Hesdin. She had a paid staff of full-time musicians in her household, too; one was a female singer named Noel, who no doubt made the Christmas festivities even brighter.

At Mahaut's castle, the Yuletide season lasted from December 25 through January 6. Besides the sounds of traditional carols, the drafty main hall was made cheerier with lots of guests, gifts, dancers dressed in deerskins, and plenty of toasts and drinking from the wassail bowl. At special feasts like these, the food itself was entertaining. Between courses, the cooks at Mahaut's castle might bring out *entremets*, which were enormous pies with real live animals (sometimes even people!) inside. Guests admired the *entremet*, rather than eating it, of course.

The countess was also an avid chess player. You wouldn't believe how emotional people got about chess back then; opponents often quarreled bitterly. In Mahaut's day, a London woman was actually stabbed to death by a sore loser! Mahaut collected chess sets, too. She had a beautiful set with silver and ivory chess pieces, and another made of crystal and jasper, a dark green stone.

This Frenchwoman's life might sound like pure fun and games, but it wasn't. Her grandfather, father, and brother were killed in the Crusades or other battles. In 1302 she inherited the large French county—or fiefdom—of Artois. This rich green region had as its borders the waters of the English Channel on one side and Belgium on another. It covered most of the area north of Paris.

When she was probably no more than twenty, she married Otho, the count of Burgundy, at that time a large region in southern France. He, too, was killed, just a year or two after they wed. Mahaut, with an infant son and daughter, was left to run both Artois and Burgundy alone from her castle capital at Hesdin.

And run them she did. Being a big landowner in medieval France was like having your own state to govern. Luckily, Mahaut had good sense, a good education, and was a wizard at math—as her orderly financial records show. As governor, mayor, judge, business manager, and law enforcement head rolled into one, she administered the villages and towns of Artois, wrote new laws, sat as a judge on civil and criminal cases, and even ran her own prisons. The city officials of Artois, long famous for its cloth and textile industry, sometimes asked for her rulings on trade agreements and other matters, too.

A conscientious ruler, Mahaut took pains to look after the welfare, health, and spiritual well-being of the people in her keeping. When she wasn't busy with other tasks, she founded monasteries and convents. She built hospitals and infirmaries. From time to time, she brought a female herbalist and spice specialist named Perronnele from Paris to Artois. Besides stocking up on medicines and herbal supplies, she asked the herbalist for advice on using them—which shows that Mahaut took a hands-on interest in health care. From her own coffers, the countess gave regular contributions to the poor, keeping track of them in her ledger books.

Mahaut was especially devoted to Saint James. Sometimes she went on religious pilgrimages, such as the trip she made with her daughter to the founding of a Paris church. At other times, she sent a religious proxy or stand-in. Over the years, she paid for various pilgrims to visit the shrine of Saint James in Compostela, Spain, where they laid her offering of silver on the altar.

Besides pleasure and pilgrimage, some of her journeys could be called "business trips." Mahaut had the responsibility of overseeing her late husband's region of Burgundy, for which she had to travel from one end of France to the other. Most of her trips were slow "official" circuits of her own domains of Artois.

When the countess neared one of her own cities or towns, she entered like a queen, at the head of a colorful procession or parade. (That was her ancient right, as reigning lady of the Artois vassals.) After the procession, the important townspeople and their families would hold lavish ceremonies, plays, and feasts in her honor. Mahaut's entry was a highlight and a holiday for the humbler folk, who cheered as her horses and her scarlet carriage came through the city gates, accompanied by jugglers, acrobats, the blast of trumpeteers, the rattle of boy drummers, and the silver jingle of harnesses. (The bigwigs might not have shared their delight—since the cost of the entry often came from their pockets.)

Countess Mahaut did have her problems, though—the main one being her nephew. The minute she inherited Artois, this young whippersnapper opposed his aunt, claiming the region for himself. At times, he actually fielded an army and attempted to oust her.

As owner of the Artois fiefdom, Mahaut had to supply military troops to the king of the land when needed. Therefore, she always maintained a standing army, to which she could add from the civilian population should trouble come up. These troops helped her put down her nephew's numerous attempts at rebellion as effectively as she won a game of chess.

With her devout nature (and her powerful family connections), you'd think that trouble with the law would be the last thing Countess Mahaut would get into. But you'd be wrong. Twice this blameless and kind woman was accused of being involved in witchcraft.

THE WITCH CRAZE IN EUROPE

For reasons not yet fully understood, a profound and terrible witch-hunting craze spread across medieval Europe, beginning in the early 1300s. Panels of religious and city officials called inquisitors set up a system to sniff out those who practiced witchcraft. These panels accused people, tortured them for confessions and the names of other witches, and put them on trial. In England, witches were hanged. In France and Germany, they were burned at the stake. Over 100,000 women eventually died. Were men accused of witchcraft too? Yes. But a mere ten to twenty percent of those accused were male. Only a few men were ever found guilty and executed.

In the first incident, a woman named Isabelle de Ferieves supposedly confessed to making a love charm for Mahaut, concocted of blood, daisies, liverwort, and vervain. Since Mahaut was a widow, and known for her piety, this was an unlikely thing for her to have ordered. The countess was known to be deeply interested in herbal remedies, however. It's very possible that her own nephew started the witchcraft rumor, hoping to obtain Artois by hook or by crook.

Isabelle was probably tortured to get her confession—the normal routine for medieval inquisitors. At the trial, Countess Mahaut was found innocent. Isabelle, however, was declared guilty. Although convicted and probably fined or whipped, at least she didn't receive a sentence of death by burning at the stake, as thousands of Frenchwomen did.

In her second run-in with the inquisitors, it appears that Mahaut herself was accused of witchcraft. Once again, she was found innocent—but the fact that a woman of her stature was accused at all gives a dark hint about the hazards of being a woman in medieval times. Mahaut might have been lucky that she lived in the early 1300s. By the 1500s, women who moved freely, thought independently, and acted fearlessly as she did became prime targets for the witch hunters of Europe.

Part Two

GERMANY
AND
ITALY

CHAPTER 5

Trotula Platearius

(ACTIVE AROUND 1080)

She was born a Ruggiero, a member of one of Salerno's well-off noble families. But Trotula wanted more than a life of ease in eleventh-century Italy. She wanted to work—a notion that must have sounded crazy to many of her kin.

When this determined girl reached her late teens, she walked into the university that was the pride of her small town, and talked people there into accepting her as a student. Not just for any career, either. She longed to become a doctor—and the Faculty of Medicine at the University of Salerno was *the* place to go. (In fact, during her day it was the only school of medicine in Europe.) Becoming a Salerno doctor was a rare feat. Becoming a female doctor was rarer still.

At the university, Trotula studied ferociously. Then as now, medical school was a major commitment. For five years, she read the works of the big names in medicine, from Hippocrates to Galen, in Latin and in Greek. She attended lectures and demonstrations. She learned how to identify and use hundreds of plants and other substances, how to grind drugs, how and when to resort to surgery. To complete her course, she did an internship (a stint of unpaid final training) with a licensed physician.

For Trotula, medicine was something she felt compelled to master. She wanted to help others—above all, she wanted to help other women. Even though her own young life had been one of comfort, she'd seen how women around her would rather suffer agonies than tell a male doctor about their problems.

More than likely it was in medical school that Trotula met John Platearius, another med student. At any rate, they married, and both became doctors. (Like much of early history, personal details about them have vanished—if they were ever written down.)

After she became Mrs. Platearius, Trotula had a house to run. After a while, she had two boys of her own to raise. Did this career

SALERNO—THE JOHNS HOPKINS OF ITS DAY

The fame of the little town of Salerno, a seaport 29 miles southeast of Naples, went back to ancient times. Long noted for its mild climate, the area also boasted mineral springs and spas. The medical school at Salerno evolved in the late 900s; soon bishops and popes came there to seek help. By Trotula's time, around 1050 to 1090, it was the Johns Hopkins of the medieval world, a place famous for the quality of its studies and its high cure rate. Crusaders returning from the Middle East were some of its best customers. Later, Salerno became part of the University of Naples; by 1400 or so, however, its medical prestige gave way to a newcomer—the university of medicine at Montpellier, France.

TROTULA'S
SECRET WEAPON—
CLEAN HANDS AND
A GOOD BEDSIDE
MANNER.

versus family dilemma make Trotula leave her work? Just the opposite. Trotula kept on practicing medicine for an ever-widening circle of patients, male and female. Eventually, it's said, she was given the university's highest honor, occupying the chair of medicine.

When her sons Matteo and John Junior grew older, they too were drawn to the healing arts. They were intensely proud of their parents. After all, very few kids in Salerno—or anywhere—could say: "My dad's a doctor—and so's my mom!"

As a doctor, Trotula was constantly trying new ways to deal with female ailments. Although she diagnosed and healed many men also, Trotula specialized in gynecology and obstetrics. She originated surgical techniques for repairing the damage to a woman's body during labor, for instance. In Trotula's day (and until the twentieth century), childbirth was a death sentence for many women. Why was it so dangerous? The main reason was infection caused by lack of cleanliness. Although she couldn't see the germs that caused infection, Trotula knew that good hygiene kept her patients from dying of childbed fever and other such ailments.

No matter how many women she saw and helped, no matter how many midwives she taught, Trotula wanted to do more. She began to write down her encyclopedic knowledge, gained over years of actual practice. In the introduction to her first book, she wrote: "Wherefore I, Trotula, pitying the calamities of women, and at the urgent request of certain ones, began to write this book on the diseases which affect females. . . ."

Her useful books (including *The Compounding of Medicaments* and *The Diseases of Women and Their Cure,* nicknamed

IS THERE A FEMALE DOCTOR IN THE HOUSE?

Shocking as the news may be to male historians, Trotula was not the only female physician at Salerno. Other women before and after her studied medicine there. They were called *Mulieres Salernitanae*—the women of Salerno. Records are scanty, but the area around Naples and Salerno long had a rich tradition of women as healers and midwives; it seems likely that at least some of their knowledge was incorporated into the curriculum. (Midwives did valuable work, but they didn't require university training.)

Girl grads of the Salerno school included surgeon and teacher Mercuriade and Francesca de Romana. Another was Sichelgaita, who liked to accompany her crusader husband onto the battlefield. She studied the "art" of poisons at Salerno—and was listed as an alumna!

Trotula Major) became incredibly popular. Her books were hand-copied, translated, and used all over Europe. (Sometimes they were plagiarized—or used without giving credit to Trotula—a fate that has often happened to female writers.)

After an English version of her book appeared, she had a new nickname in England: "Dame Trot." Nursery rhymes and famous poems like Chaucer's *Canterbury Tales* mentioned her by name. When the printing press came into being, 400 years after Dr. Platearius's death, one of the earliest volumes printed in Italian was *The Diseases of Women*. A few early copies of Trotula's books still exist in England, Spain, Germany, Austria, and other countries.

Eventually, even the most humble traveling herbalists used her books as reference. They would boast of being Trotula's disciples as they set up shop on street corners in France, Belgium, and Italy.

At some point, the doctors of Salerno's medical school also put together a how-to encyclopedia of medicine and well-being. Trotula and her husband John were invited to contribute, of course. That encyclopedia, written in simple verse for ordinary folks, went through 20 editions, achieving what we would call best-seller status for at least five centuries.

We don't know when or how Dr. Trotula died. But tradition says that the people of Salerno mourned her greatly, and honored her with a funeral procession that wound for two miles through the little city.

Hildegard of Bingen

(1098-1179)

H ildegard was about three years old when she had her first vision. She recalled later, "I saw a great light, and my soul quaked . . . being a child, I could not reveal it." The visions occurred again; bewildered by her powers, this young daughter of a German knight told no one. But Mechthilde and Hildebert, her mother and father, noticed that their daughter was different. Besides Hildegard's uncanny ability to see things others didn't, she was the tenth child in the family—the baby, and often sickly.

"We'll tithe her to God," her parents decided. Tithing, or giving a tenth part of whatever you owned to the church, was something every pious Christian in the eleventh century tried to do—although people usually tithed money or crops, rather than children.

When Hildegard turned eight, her parents took her to the Benedictine monastery of Mount St. Disibode and gave her to the

HILDEGARDE

church as an anchoress (a religious recluse who was locked away from the world). All eyes were on Hildegard during the long ceremony, eerily similar to a funeral. Dressed in their finest, her mother and father attended, as did important friends and relations. In a gloomy, torch-lit room about the size of a breakfast nook, a choir sang hymns, while monks recited the words that would keep the eight-year-old locked up for life. Then everyone left, the priest gave a final blessing, and the door to Hildegard's small room, called a cell, was physically blocked up.

The little girl didn't find herself completely alone, however. Already living in her cell was another anchoress named Jutta, who'd agreed to become her teacher.

Anchoress cells weren't that different from prison cells. (Some prison cells might seem luxurious in comparison!) Sanitation facilities usually consisted of a bucket, removed daily. In other situations, the occupants got to leave the cell a few minutes a day to visit an outside privy. We don't know what the setup for Hildegard and Jutta was. Exercise, fresh air—even light—were in short supply. Most cells had just one window, small and open for certain hours only. Their food was passed through the window.

A typical day for them began at 2 A.M., with the sound of the monks chanting matins or morning services. At first light, and later at sunrise, Hildegard could hear (but not see) the monks sing the religious chants called lauds and prime. Then Jutta began lessons. Hildegard learned to read and write from the Psalter (the book commonly used for beginners), and a bit of Latin. She also learned to play the psaltery, a 10-stringed harp. Hildegard loved music, and could always carry a tune—or invent one.

WHEN RELIGION WAS THE ONLY GAME IN TOWN—BESIDES MARRIAGE

As a European medieval miss, about the only way you had of getting an education—and of getting out of a marriage arranged by your parents—was to join a religious order. After paying a dowry or fee to the religious order of your choice, you could take vows and become a nun, living in a convent. Or you could adopt the life of an anchoress, which normally meant retiring to a tiny cell or cave for a life of chastity, simplicity, and solitude. (Men also did this; they were called anchorites.)

In the fourteenth century, the Beguine movement arose in Europe. It allowed women of more modest means to lead a religious life. To enter a Beguinage or communal house for beguines, you didn't need a dowry. This spiritual refuge housed women who took vows that weren't as severe as in the convent. Beguine women also worked in the community, tending the sick and doing much other work of value.

Around noon in winter, the little girl and her teacher ate their only meal of the day—usually two cooked dishes, like beans or eggs, plus fruit and vegetables when available, and bread. The Benedictines didn't stint on bread: everybody got a pound of it daily! In summer, Hildegard ate both a midday meal and a light evening supper. She and Jutta washed down their meals with beer or wine—rarely water.

By the time she was 15, the visions and spiritual gifts of Jutta's pupil became common knowledge. Nuns and other women looking for religious inspiration wanted to study with her. Since Hildegard couldn't leave her cell, they crowded into her quarters for lessons. At some point, the head of the monastery saw the contradiction. Neither Jutta nor Hildegard was living the enclosed and solitary life of an anchoress. He decided to let Hildegard take the veil of a nun—and made Jutta the head of this new convent of religious women. As nuns, they lived in the same holy way, but had more freedom of movement.

For over twenty years, until Jutta died in 1136, Hildegard studied, prayed, and thought about God and the message of Christianity. She was content to have Jutta as leader of their community, while she tended her herb garden and treated the sick with remedies she devised. Even after being elected the new administrative head after Jutta's death, she remained quiet and humble.

All that changed in 1141. Hildegard was bowled over by a tremendous vision. "The heavens were opened, and a blinding light of exceptional brilliance flowed through my entire brain," she recalled. "It kindled my heart and breast like a flame, not burning but warming . . . and suddenly I was able to taste of the understanding of books."

God commanded her to write down her visions—but for several years, she hesitated. Then Hildegard fell seriously ill. Finally, at age forty-three, she began work on *Scivias,* or *Know the Ways,* her first book of revelations. Her strength returned as she worked. When he saw part of the manuscript, the pope himself encouraged Hildegard to finish it. With the help of Volmar, the monk who acted as her secretary, she completed the book in ten years.

Hildegard also had dazzling artistic visions—and she wanted them to accompany her writing. Most likely she didn't hold the brushes herself, but gave very detailed instruction to the illuminators (illustrators, we would call them) for *Scivias.* She probably had more than one artistic helper; they could have been monks as well as nuns. Color by color and image by image, she would describe her vision. Only when Hildegard was satisfied with the painting would she go on to the next. There were thirty-five in all, each described by her in words and images of flaming power, terror, and beauty. She used the symbol of a fiery dog to stand for humans who bite at their own condition. A reddish lion stood for the misery of war; a giant worm, for evil and human pollution. A circle of shimmering blue represented the living fire of God.

Granger Collection, #GR4371. Used with permission.

Then Hildegard took on another immense project. The nunnery at St. Disibode had gotten too small and cramped for her women. Over the sharp protests of the monks, she founded another convent at Bingen, about twenty miles north. Located on a hill overlooking the lush green banks of the Rhine River, this convent she named after Rupert, a Celtic saint. Her departure upset the monks at Disibode for money motives, as well as spiritual ones. Upon leaving Disibode, the nuns took their dowries with them. (When a girl entered the convent and became a bride of Christ, her parents paid a dowry, just as if she were marrying a mortal man.)

From the start, Hildegard, now consecrated an abbess by the archbishop, found life at Rupertsberg exhilarating, despite its drawbacks. At first, the nuns lived in temporary structures. Besides that hardship, the fifty sisters were running what amounted to a guest house. Pilgrims and guests kept showing up, wanting to meet the abbess. Little by little, however, the monastery got built; it even came to have luxuries, such as piped-in water. (Hildegard's growing celebrity, and her speaking abilities, brought in more and more donations, which paid for the construction.)

Hildegard plunged into a variety of projects. Besides founding a third monastery for thirty more nuns in 1165, she composed music and lyrics for seventy-seven liturgical pieces. She wrote *Play of the Virtues,* a morality play, and poetry. Drawing on her interests in botany and healing, she wrote a fantastic encyclopedia, describing nearly five hundred herbs, plants, and medicinal remedies.

As she grew older, she became bolder. A political and religious activist, she lobbied hard against the increasing corruption of the clergy in her times. In pursuit of her beliefs, she fired off hundreds of letters to popes, princesses, and humbler folk.

In her seventies, she even took to the road, preaching around Germany, Switzerland, and France about the need for reform in the church. Hildegard didn't care about winning new friends, or alienating old ones. She argued with the emperor of the Holy Roman Empire. She challenged her archbishop, who tried to punish her. She called one pope "timid," and in the year before she died at age eighty-one, had a showdown with another over the case of an excommunicated youth. (She won the argument, too.)

There was no end to her creativity. During nearly forty years of creative outpourings, Hildegard invented over 850 new words. One of her loveliest terms seems especially relevant today. She thought of God's love, the physical world, and the perfect human state as being juicy, green, and ever renewing—like the new buds on the grapevines and the spring grasses of her homeland in the Rhine Valley. To capture that idea, she invented the word *viriditas*, or greening power—a word that also expresses the "evergreen" quality of Hildegard herself.

CHAPTER 7

Clare Scifi of Assisi

(ABOUT 1193-1252)

For years before Clare was born, her mother Ortolana couldn't seem to get pregnant. She'd made pilgrimages to shrines around Italy to pray for a child. Finally, desperate, she begged her husband Favarone, the Count of Sasso, to let her visit the holiest place of all. He said yes; so with her cousin, she made the long journey from Assisi to Jerusalem.

When she got home, she conceived at last. But Ortolana was nervous. Daily she walked from her lavish house on the Piazza San Rufino, across the square into the cool dark cathedral of Assisi. There she prayed for her baby's safety. One day a voice spoke to her: "Don't be afraid—you'll bring forth a clear light that will illuminate the world."

When the baby came, Ortolana and her husband had no trouble naming her. "We'll call her Chiara," they said. "The Shining One." (Chiara is Clare in English.)

Clare shone forth, even as a youngster. She was very tall for a girl. Her name turned out to be a perfect fit; she had a shining waterfall of long blonde hair—a rare sight, even in northern Italy. Her parents were rich and indulgent; if Clare wanted a pearl or a dress of silk, she got it.

As Clare grew, so did the family. Suddenly, Ortolana was producing plenty of siblings for Clare. Her baby brother didn't live long, but she soon had a girl gang of kid sisters as well as cousins, who did everything together.

When Clare grew into a teenager, her relatives got busy matchmaking. As everyone said, their beautiful blonde was one of the marital catches in the area. The Scifis (no, it's not pronounced sci-fi, as in science fiction!) moved in the highest circles of Assisi society. Besides the town house, the family had castles in the lush countryside.

Clare might have looked soft, but she had a will as hard as diamond. Over family protests, she learned to read, speak some Latin, and skillfully dodge would-be suitors. She turned fifteen without marrying. Then sixteen. At seventeen, her uncle said to her father, "It's high time that young lady was married," and brought his own candidate around the house. Clare turned him down flat.

Not long afterwards, Clare went to church—and there, preaching the sermon, was Francis, an older local man she'd heard many bizarre things about. For years he'd had a reputation for wild party behavior with his friends. But by the time Clare was in her teens, he'd become a holy man: rebelling against his wealthy family, going barefoot, repairing the crumbling churches of Assisi with stones and money he'd begged, even preaching naked! He already had followers, too—including two of Clare's male cousins.

The words Francis preached in church that day, and his sincerity, touched her heart. Clare was overwhelmed. With the help of her sisters, Clare began to meet secretly with Francis. For months, messages and intense plans flew back and forth.

On March 18, 1212, Clare went with her family to celebrate Palm Sunday. She wore her favorite satin dress and her finest jew-

LOVER OF LARKS—AND LEPERS

Born Giovanni Bernadone, the son of well-to-do textile merchants, Francis had a thin face, a swarthy complexion, and jug ears. For twenty-five years, he danced, partied with his friends, and blew his folks' money on food, drink, and lavish, often strange clothing. Then Francis spent a year as a prisoner of war; that gave him time to contemplate, and it changed him from ne'er-do-well to a holy man. After his call from God, Francis adopted a life of poverty and founded the Franciscan order of friars. Known for his love of animals, he preached sermons to birds and wolves and cared for people with leprosy. Europe at that time had thousands of leper houses, where sufferers of this disfiguring skin disease were looked after by those who cared— like Francis.

Archive Photos, ID#41646. Used with permission.

els to church that day. That night, she ran away from home. Clare left by a special side door, the one the family used only to remove someone in the household who had died. It was a fitting choice for the death of her old life, and the beginning of a new one.

When she rendezvoused with Francis, he and the local bishop quickly took her to the Chapel of Saint Mary of the Angels. There, kneeling on the dirt floor of the chapel, she took vows of poverty, chastity, and obedience. Standing above her, Francis lifted Clare's golden hair and cut it off at the scalp. It fell in a heap, making a gleaming offering to God.

Clare put on a rough brown habit like the one that Francis and his followers, called Franciscans, wore. She tied it with a rope around her waist and put on wooden sandals. She didn't need the fancy dress and shoes she'd discarded with her hair. Embracing this new life of simplicity and poverty, she felt clothed in glory.

Her parents were, as expected, outraged. Her sisters, on the other hand, were tickled. Soon Clare's 15-year-old sister Agnes ran away from her fiancé to join the Franciscans, followed by Clare's cousin Pacifica. Finally, an armed band of angry Scifi males went after their female family members. Legend has it that they were turned away by Clare's convincing words—and by a small miracle. As they dragged Agnes with them, she became heavier than lead; finally, no matter how many men tried, they just could not carry her away.

Clare and the other young women went to live in the small stone church convent of San Damiano. Clare's life of contemplation and her holy example soon attracted other women to join the Poor Clares or the Little Sisters, as the order came to be known. Even her own mother would later enter the order.

For years, Clare fasted completely on Mondays, Wednesdays, and Fridays, during Lent, and on other holy days. The rest of the time, she ate trifling amounts. She didn't need physical nourishment, she said; she got it from her spiritual life. Physically denying and punishing the body was looked on as proof of holiness in Clare's day.

At length she became gravely ill from her religious anorexia. In front of the other sisters, Francis said to her, "I must insist that you eat at least an ounce and a half of bread each day!" Clare recognized she'd taken things too far. When she became abbess of the Poor Clares in 1216, she advised her women to balance fasting with common sense. As she explained in a later letter to one of her followers: "Our bodies are not bronze, and our strength isn't granite. We're frail and inclined to every weakness. So I beg you to moderate the exaggerated and impossible fasting I know you've started. That way, your sacrifice will always be seasoned with the salt of common sense."

Clare's religious commitment made her a wonderful role model and leader for the women in her order, which spread throughout Italy, and eventually into other countries. She even became a counselor to popes.

Six different times, bishops and other church officials wrote a set of official rules for the Poor Clares and tried to impose them—

THE FRANCISCANS AND THE POOR CLARES

A preacher visiting Italy around 1216 marveled at the number of people who had "left the world" and become Franciscans or Poor Clares. The Franciscans took vows of poverty, begged for their food, owned nothing, preached the word of God, and did social work in their local communities each day. In 1216, the Poor Clares may also have worked some of the time in cities and towns, like the Franciscan friars did. Later, however, the Poor Clares chose to become cloistered, remaining within their convent. To support themselves, they sewed altar cloths and raised a few vegetables in their garden. Clare herself spent the rest of her life inside San Damiano. Clare had a simple philosophy. She thought of poverty as a high privilege—the best way she knew to do God's will.

but none accurately echoed Clare's beliefs. In September of 1252, Clare sat down and wrote her own rules for the religious community and sent them to the pope for approval. Time dragged; now sixty years old, Clare got sick once more. Bedridden, she wondered: Would she ever hear from the pope? Finally, on August 9 of the following year, she received official word. The Poor Clares would be governed by her notion of the privilege of poverty.

She kissed the document many times. Two days after Clare read the pope's letter, surrounded by nuns and family, she slipped peacefully away, saying, "I am speaking to my own happy soul."

Just two years after Clare died, this gentle woman was made a saint. The pope's words about her still ring through the centuries: "O Clare, endowed with so many titles of clarity! Clear even before your conversion, clearer in your manner of living, exceedingly clear in your enclosed life, and brilliant in splendor after the course of your mortal life. In Clare, a clear mirror is given to the entire world."

A SAINT FOR SORE EYES

Officially known in the Catholic Church as the "protector of embroiderers," Clare was also made the patron saint of television in 1958 by Pope Pius the Twelfth. This stems from the story that Clare, sick in bed one Christmas, was unable to attend midnight Mass—yet heard the singing and saw the manger of Jesus set up in the chapel, on her wall. Clare is also prayed to by Catholics who have sore eyes. This is because she once nursed Saint Francis, who stayed at San Damiano when his eyes gave him terrible pain from time to time.

At San Damiano Church in Assisi, the small garden of flowers begun so long ago by Clare still blooms. And in the church, another memento of the Shining One is carefully treasured—Clare's long blonde tresses, cut off as a gift to God.

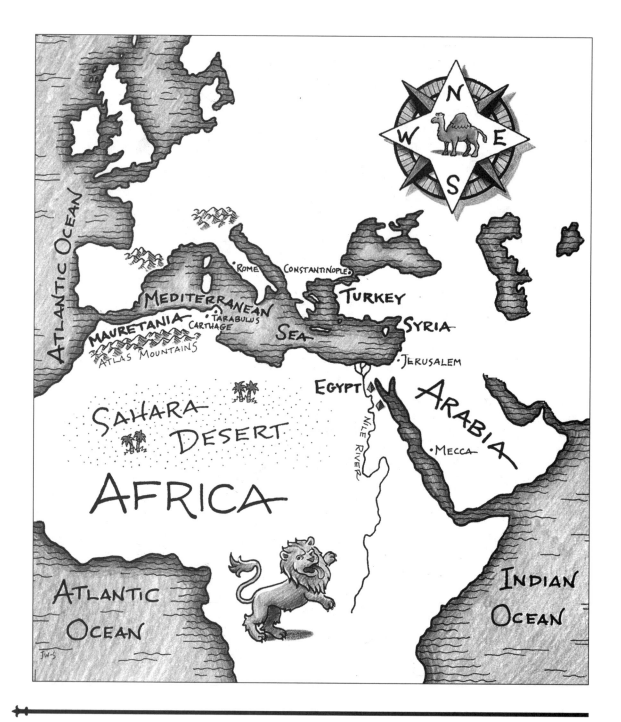

Part Three

MIDDLE EAST
AND NORTH
AFRICA

Khadija bint Khuwaylid

(5 5 5 - 6 1 9)

Fourteen hundred years ago, a confident woman named Khadija bint Khuwaylid took stock of her life. At forty, she'd gotten nearly everything she wanted. She came from a family of wealth, breeding, and connections. Head of her own international import-export business, she had a terrific job that gave her joy and independence of movement. True, she was a widow now, but she'd had the love of two husbands. And she lived in Mecca, the loveliest city in Arabia, and the best hometown she could ask for.

Then she met Mohammed, a handsome man in his mid-twenties. He came to her attention as a job applicant.

"Could you take charge of the trade caravan and the goods I'm sending to Syria?" she asked. His curly black hair and beard were beautifully groomed, and he had the clearest, most penetrating eyes she'd ever seen.

He looked closely at Khadija; besides her aristocratic good

looks, she had a comfortable air of command he found very attractive. "I'd be happy to."

Khadija checked with the traders Mohammed had worked for. To a man, they said he was honest, reliable, and shrewd. She learned he was a native of Mecca, orphaned young; he became a shepherd at twelve, later learning the caravan business. Although his reputation was excellent, his finances weren't. In fact, he'd already asked a local girl to marry him and been rejected by her father.

As soon as Mohammed returned from his first job assignment to Syria, Khadija met with him. The goods he had escorted on camelback across the desert, he'd been able to trade for other more costly items, doubling her investment. This financial triumph made her happy. But profit seemed small, compared with her delight at seeing him again.

Khadija was a good judge of character. And she knew her heart. "Mohammed, I want to marry you," she said. (Another account says that she sent an intermediary to Mohammed with her proposal. Either way, it was a bold action, rarely seen in seventh-century Arabia!)

Mohammed said yes. Besides marrying what she represented—wealth, family connections, a comfortable lifestyle he had not known before—the simple fact was: he loved her.

The couple had big issues to overcome. The difference in their ages was one. Probably more difficult than the age gap was the fact that Khadija was her husband's boss, and her wealth supported them. But they worked things out.

Despite being forty, Khadija was thrilled to find herself quickly pregnant. And then pregnant again—six times in all. In between the births of two sons and four daughters, she continued to run her trading caravans. Now a merchant, Mohammed went on extended trading trips throughout the Middle East. He worked very hard for their company; the two of them became even more prosperous.

About 610, when they'd been married some fifteen years, Mohammed began a spiritual search. With Khadija's blessing—and occasional companionship—he would go off to meditate. His travels as a merchant had been an eye-opener. From Christian monks and Jewish holy men, he'd learned about other peoples who followed one god. In contrast, the society in which he and Khadija lived still worshipped a variety of gods and images, including a sacred shrine in Mecca called the Ka'aba.

THE KA'ABA: A MESSAGE FROM THE HEAVENS

Eons ago, the Arabian desert got a visitor from space. Unlike most meteors, it did not burn up before embedding itself in the sand. Awed natives found a large piece of shiny black stone. Later, the stone became a shrine, and the city of Mecca grew up around it. The shrine's keepers were families like Khadija's, who became rich and powerful as a result. After Mohammed the Prophet founded Islam, he made the worship of the Ka'aba part of Islam. Today the sacred stone is part of a cube-shaped shrine, hidden from direct view by a billowing curtain. Only Muslims on pilgrimage to Mecca are permitted near. As part of their *haj* or pilgrimage, they walk five times around the Ka'aba.

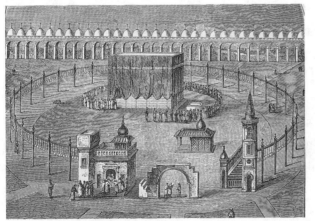

Archive Photos, #51373. Used with permission.

One day, while meditating in his favorite cave on Mount Hiraa, Mohammed heard the voice of an angel, commanding him to read and recite the word of God. When he came to himself, he ran straight home to his wife to share his revelations with her.

Khadija was joyful; her husband had been singled out by Allah (the Arabic word for God) to become his prophet.

With his wife's encouragement, Mohammed accepted his call from Allah. He would spend his life spreading the word of this new religion he called "Islam," meaning "submission to God's will." His partner in everything, Khadija became one of his first converts. She was now a Muslim—a word that means "one who submits."

For nine years, Mohammed preached, struggling hard to win followers, while Khadija kept the kids fed, the home fires burning, and the business running. Besides being his marital partner, she was his confidante, his religious student, and his disciple in spreading the word of Islam. With a wife like her, it's not surprising that Mohammed advocated education and legal rights for women as a key part of Islam.

By 619, their Muslim community, while very small, was a reality. Khadija, however, was now sixty-four, and her life had run its course. She met death calmly; fifty-year-old Mohammed was devastated, however. Even the presence of his four surviving children failed to cheer him.

"Men and women are equal as two teeth in a comb," Mohammed had often said. That equality was the kind of partnership that he and Khadija were blessed with. Although Islam evolved greatly after Khadija's death, that saying was one of many that would later appear in the *hadith,* the traditional collection of sayings and stories from Mohammed the Prophet.

Damia al-Kahina

(ACTIVE AROUND 680)

For those who lived among the endless golden sand dunes and the stony wastelands of the Sahara Desert, there was nothing more important than water. In a way, it was fitting that Damia al-Kahina, a freedom fighter for the nomadic peoples of North Africa, died fighting near an Algerian well that's still called "bir al Kahinah" in her honor.

The child of nomad parents, Damia probably called a black wool tent home. Born somewhere in North Africa, she loved the silent sea of dunes that rolled across the vast Sahara. Historians argue about Damia's ethnic origins. Some say she was a Berber girl, from one of the tribes that had lived for centuries in the high Atlas Mountains overlooking the coast of what we would call Morocco today. Others think it's more likely that Damia was a member of a Jewish tribe, one of many small bands that had wandered across the lands and sands of North Africa for millennia.

Little is known about her younger days, but writers of the time often mentioned her "flashing good looks." Like other nomadic women of her time and place, Damia probably had skin the color of coffee with cream, small blue tattoos on her chin and forehead, and dark eyes, made more dramatic by being lined with kohl. Her body was swathed in robes of snowy white or pale blue. Her head was protected from sun and wind by a turban of cloth, decorated with beads and silver coins. From her belt hung a silver dagger, the shape of the moon at its quarter.

By the time Damia reached the age of marriage, she was also celebrated for her evident courage and her uncanny powers of intuition and prophecy. Many even called her a sorceress or a diviner

THE NOMADIC TRIBES OF NORTH AFRICA

The Berbers, the original inhabitants of North Africa, have occupied these lands since prehistoric times. Some Berbers settled into town life. But most preferred the wandering life of the nomad, moving in camel caravans and sleeping in tents under the sharp stars of the desert night. North Africa was also home to Jewish nomads. No one knew where they came from, or when. Some thought they began to wander through Arabia and then to North Africa in the seventh century B.C. Over the centuries, they mixed with the Berbers, eventually adopting their language and some of their customs. The Jewish nomads kept their faith, however. On holy days, a Jewish nomad (as Damia probably was) would take care to keep her dagger in its sheath. Like the Berbers, the wandering Jewish tribes loved poetry and song and spent the year traveling from one grazing place to another, sometimes stopping to plant a crop.

who could predict the future. (Some accounts say that "kahina" means "diviner.")

Becoming a mother didn't change her much. We know nothing of her husband; she had two sons and raised them, meanwhile becoming al-Kahina or chieftain of her tribe. (Sometimes the tribe itself is called Kahina; other accounts call it the Zenata or Jerua tribe.)

Already strong, with Damia at its head the Kahina tribe came to dominate most of the other tribes, Jewish and Berber alike, in North Africa. Diplomatic Damia had a unique recruiting policy. She made friends with even the most remote tribes; she asked for

and got the support of even the touchiest leaders. This strong woman added to her power base in a novel way, too. She took in refugees, including the large number of Jews who'd been driven out of Spain, starting around 580, by the Visigoths.

This political and military leader of the seventh century really knew how to bring very different people together in a common cause. Her army came to have both Jewish and Christian soldiers; it also included Berber tribesmen and fighters from Mauritania, which the Arabs called Maghrib, or land of the sunset. (Today that part of Morocco is still called Maghreb.)

Jealous rivals and would-be male leaders called their female chieftain power-hungry. The truth of the matter was, Damia was hungry for something else: freedom. She clearly saw that her coalition of people would soon have a formidable opponent. From faraway Arabia, moving almost as swiftly as a hungry flock of migrating birds, Islamic armies were closing in on the north coast of Africa.

"Convert the infidels!" they shouted as they marched. Just seventy years earlier, Mohammed the Prophet had founded the religion of Islam. He, and later his successors, encouraged Muslims to spread the message of Islam through what was called *jihad,* or holy war.

For a time, Damia watched as the Arabs swept through nearby lands. In 687, the invaders won a major battle. An army led by Egyptian Prince Hassan conquered Carthage, the great city on the North African coast. While the victors were busy executing the city's Byzantine leaders and establishing a brand-new city called Tunis nearby, Prince Hassan sat in his tent and met with his military advisers.

"Soon all of North Africa will be ours!" one gloated.

"All that remains is to crush the Kahina, and the rest of the tribes will fall," said another. "And it is led by a woman—how difficult could that be?"

The military men laughed. Prince Hassan laughed hardest. "I think we can take our time," he said.

Damia al-Kahina picked that moment to strike. Sweeping down from the mountains, she and her troops savagely cut the Muslim armies into ribbons, driving them farther and farther east. At length, the tatters of the invading army limped into Egypt. Prince Hassan scuttled to get away, just like the rest. Only then did Damia call off her tribes.

After a great feast to celebrate the victory, Damia settled in to an even tougher task: to govern. For five years, she ruled 1,500 miles of North Africa, from the sunny shores of Mauretania (Morocco today) off the Atlantic coast to the city of Tarabulus (today called Tripoli) in the sands of Libya. Until the twentieth century, she was the only ruler—male or female—ever to control that vast area politically.

To do so, she had to be tough. Maybe she was too tough: people began to complain about her harsh rule and swift punishments. "She is harder on us than on the enemy," the landowners grumbled. Some of them began to think twice about their alliances.

Some think she wasn't tough enough. In 703, the mercy she'd shown by not annihilating Prince Hassan and his army came back to haunt her. Hassan gathered another army and began to march from Egypt west into her lands.

This time, Damia saw her support slipping. Some of her Christian allies sent out negotiating feelers to the invaders. Her Jewish allies, unhappy that Damia also had Christians and Berbers in her coalition, began to back away. So she tried another strategy. It was a cruel move, born of desperation. "We shall make the land so inhospitable that the invaders cannot survive," she said to the chiefs of each tribe in her alliance.

"What does she mean?" the Berbers, the Jewish tribespeople, and other inhabitants of North Africa asked one another. They soon saw.

Damia ordered her forces to set fire to the cities and to burn the defensive forts. They cut down the cool groves of pomegranates and fruit orchards. They left oases without a single date palm standing. They salted the fertile fields where grain and vegetables had grown, so they became barren as the burning sand.

Horrified and angry, her own people and the coalitions she had worked so hard to bring together began to desert to the Muslim invaders. This gave help and hope to Prince Hassan, who refused to retreat and kept up his siege.

Just before the final battle that would take her life, Damia had the wisdom to see that her moment in history was up. She counseled her two sons, now grown and with her army: "Surrender to the Muslims, my children—perhaps they will show you mercy."

To the surprise of many, that's just what Prince Hassan did. Her sons eventually served in Hassan's army, and even converted to Islam; one son was part of the Islamic army that crossed over to conquer Spain in 711.

But Damia's desert spirit of religious and cultural freedom did not die entirely. From the seventh century until modern times, small bands of nomadic Jews who proudly claimed descent from Kahina continued to live deep in the Atlas Mountains. In 1948, 1,200 years after the Diviner lived and died, the remnants of al-Kahina's band were resettled in the new state of Israel.

CHAPTER 10

Anna Comnena

(1083–AROUND 1148)

The First Crusade, which began on August 15, 1096, wasn't reported in any newspaper. It did, however, have an eyewitness reporter to document it—Anna Comnena. A princess of the Byzantine Empire, Anna was the oldest child of Empress Irene and Emperor Alexius I. She lived in Constantinople, the city we now call Istanbul.

The Crusades were often made out to be noble pilgrimages by fair and gallant knights, traveling from Europe to take back the holy city of Jerusalem from the infidels. Anna Comnena knew better. She saw the crusaders in action. Many of them were unwelcome, unwashed, and ungallant invaders who came for reasons far from holy.

Anna's father was one of the key people who got the First Crusade off the ground. Ambitious Alexius was very short of manpower, and anxious to reconquer Turkey, Syria, and other lands once governed by his Byzantine Empire. He decided to ask the

THERE WERE
SHOPPING SPREES AND
MOTHER-DAUGHTER
DRESS-ALIKES IN
ANNA'S DAY, TOO.

pope in Rome for troops. "Send us help," he said to Pope Urban. "The infidels (he meant non-Christians, mainly Muslims) are nearly at our door. Together let's chase them out of these lands—and from Christianity's holy places!"

The pope liked this SOS from Alexius. It gave him an excuse to form a papal army. "A holy war!" he declared. "It's our duty to march to the rescue of the Christians in the East." To make the Crusade more attractive to Europeans, the pope proclaimed that anyone could do penance for sins by fighting the holy war, or giving money to it. "What about taking lives?" people asked. Officials had a good answer for that, too. It would only be a sin if Christians were killed, they said.

Soon Anna heard the bad news about the "Franks," as she and her fellow Byzantines called the Europeans. To Anna and her family, the Franks were barely civilized. Anna's father wasn't happy about the troops that were being sent to him, either. "Instead of the trained soldiers I asked for, the pope has gotten everyone stirred up!" he exclaimed.

Religious enthusiasm soon got completely out of hand. The first wave to arrive in Constantinople was a motley crew of untrained peasants, French and German, plus a few foot soldiers and knights, who'd already attacked and killed four thousand innocent Hungarians along the way. They were led by a fanatic monk riding a donkey who called himself Peter the Hermit. (Anna nicknamed him "Cuckoo Peter.")

As the summer heat shimmered off the walls of Anna's city, thousands of people milled around. The singing, chanting crusaders, the boiling dust they raised, the long slender palm branches and crosses they carried, made a tremendous impression on the princess. From her perch atop the great stone walls of Constantinople, Anna saw it all: "Full of ardor and enthusiasm, the Franks thronged every highway. With these warriors came a host of civilians, outnumbering the grains of sand on the seashore, carrying palms in their hands and bearing crosses on their shoulders. There were women and children, too, who had left their own countries. Like tributaries joining a river, they streamed in all directions toward us."

It was a terrifying logistics problem. These ragtag arrivals were short on food, water, and good behavior. And behind them were eighty thousand more crusaders, led by powerful princes from the west. Besides supplying food and water, and helping with the big job of transporting them across the waters of the Bosphorus that divided Constantinople in two, Anna's father was worried

CRAZY ABOUT CROSSBOWS AND GREEK FIRE

Unlike most girls, Anna Comnena was deeply interested in military matters. She knew the details of every battle her dad ever fought. She studied the workings of the crossbow, and marveled at this invention of the barbarians. She vividly described "Greek fire," the Byzantine secret weapon that vomited flames from a cannon—without giving away its formula. In the nine hundred years that have passed since Anna described Greek fire, no one has yet figured out the secret ingredients of this military mystery.

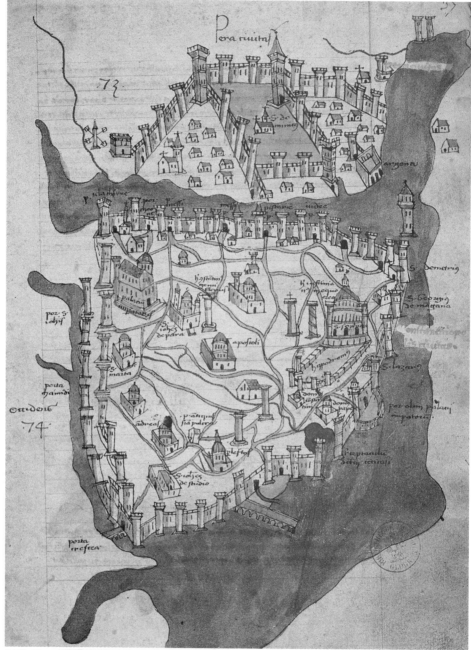

Art Resource, #S0073714#PF1228. Used with permission.

HIGH
WALLS STILL
SURROUND
ANNA'S HOME
CITY—BUT NOW
IT'S CALLED
ISTANBUL.

about violence. He'd seen the Franks in action already. As Anna later wrote, "He feared the incursions of these people, for he had already experienced the savage fury of their attack, their fickleness of mind, and their readiness to approach anything with violence."

Anna thought it would take a miracle to move the waves of crusaders through Constantinople and get them safely on their way. As it turned out, the flood of people headed for Jerusalem lasted nine months.

A teen when the First Crusade began, Anna was twenty-four when it ended. Jerusalem was now in Christian hands. As predicted, countless knights and civilians had straggled back into the Queen of Cities, as Constantinople was nicknamed. Many were hurt, ill, or simply destitute. Anna worked with her father to establish and run an enormous hospital and convalescent center in the heart of Constantinople. Called the Orphanage, it had special facilities for the mutilated, the blind, and the poor. As many as ten thousand lived there, it was guessed. As Anna wrote, "The buildings stood in a double circle . . . so large was the circle that if you wished to visit these people and started early in the morning, it would be evening before you were done."

The hours she spent at the Orphanage were not a make-work job to occupy the spare time of a princess. Anna had a natural talent for medicine, brought along by a fabulous education. She'd studied the wisdom and literature of the ancient Greeks and Romans. She'd tackled geometry, mathematics, astronomy, and medicine. As a cultured Byzantine princess, naturally she knew the Christian scriptures well, played music and sang acceptably, and had an understanding of geography and history.

An all-around intellectual, Anna had formidable skills as a healer. She followed the teachings of Galen, the renowned physician and teacher of Roman days. She also understood the effects of the mind on the body. When her father became ill with the gout, she began to research that disease and its possible cures. Eventually she wrote a book about it. Later in life, when her father was on his deathbed, she was called in as one of the medical experts.

A bookworm since childhood, Anna Comnena was, sad to say, consumed by another worm as well. It was called jealousy. Anna always craved the family limelight. In 1091, eight-year-old Anna had been the center of attention. With great pomp, she became engaged to Constantine Ducas, the boy who would inherit the throne from her father. After a momentous ceremony, she went to live in the palace of her new fiancé's family, as was the custom.

Then, like a series of slaps to her face, dreadful events began to happen. Without warning, her five-year-old brother John was named the new heir; Anna's engagement with Constantine was abruptly broken off by one or both sides; and Constantine died in 1097.

Angry and feeling cheated, Anna was married off that same year to Nicephorus Bryennius. She was fourteen. She grumbled at the time, "I would prefer to remain unwed." Nicephorus was as nice as his name, however. Handsome, hardworking, and a whiz on the battlefield, he made points with Anna's dad and little by little, with Anna herself. They had four children together and many years of marriage before he died from illness. Despite the happiness she enjoyed with her family, Anna's heart still looked for revenge.

When her beloved father died in 1118, brilliant Anna gave in to her dark side. Twice she devised plots and conspired with others to assassinate her brother John, now Emperor of the Byzantine Empire. When the plots failed, John forgave his big sister. But Anna didn't get away scot-free. John banished her from the court and exiled her to a nunnery.

Oddly enough, out of her punishment and her continuing bitterness came a wonderful legacy. Now in her late thirties, Anna Comnena put her mind to a new labor—one that would occupy the rest of her life. She began to write *The Alexiad,* a history of her father and her family. Sheer luck decreed that Anna's book survived the lottery of time. In *The Alexiad,* we have more than a family memoir. *The Alexiad* is a precious, sometimes melodramatic account of the Byzantine world of the eleventh and twelfth centuries. It shows the Crusades from the perspective of a woman, a civilian, and a keen-eyed reporter who saw and remembered it all.

Part Four

THE FAR EAST

KYONG-JU—MUCH MORE THAN A BUMP IN THE ROAD

For seven centuries, the Silla queens and kings lived—and died—in incredible luxury. Today the Korean city of Kyong-ju is surrounded by their massive burial mounds, the shape and color of giant camel humps. Archaeologists have found tens of thousands of artifacts in them, from gold and jade tiger-claw earrings to a marvelous painting of a flying horse, done on birchbark. Visitors can actually walk into some of the tombs; many of the finds stand in the open air. Others, including things from Sonduk's reign, can be seen in the splendid Kyong-ju Museum.

Sonduk of Korea

(ABOUT 610-647)

Every seventh-century Korean girl carried a *changdo* in her pocket, a knife used to peel fruit—and to protect her virtue, if need be. Young Sonduk, who had an inquiring mind, also found her knife handy on outdoor field trips. When her father, the king of Silla, wanted to find her, he knew where to look. Nine times out of ten, his daughter would be outdoors, lying on the grasses and trying to get eye to eye with a grasshopper, or cutting open the egg casing of a spider. Sitting as still as a Buddhist monk, she would watch the nature around her for hours—just so she could see how the flowers opened. At night, she loved to gaze at the stars moving over the pagodas and rooftops of Kyong-ju, her capital city.

One day, she came running into the palace, her long shiny black braid flapping behind her. The king had just received a package from a very important person: the ruler of Korea's big neighbor, China. Sonduk crowded in close to see what was inside the package. Unwrapped, it turned out to be several beautiful paintings of peony flowers, the symbols of nobility and wealth. With them was a smaller packet, containing a peony seed. Everyone gathered around to admire the gifts.

"What do you think of the paintings, daughter?" the king asked Sonduk.

"Very pretty," said Sonduk. "But it's too bad the flowers don't smell as good as they look."

"How do you know that, daughter?" he asked, puzzled.

Sonduk stared at him with her sharp black eyes. Grown-ups missed the most obvious things! "If the peonies had fragrance, dad," she answered, "there would be bees and butterflies around them in the paintings."

The adults around the king were amused. What would come out of this outspoken seven-year-old's mouth next?

Intrigued, Sonduk's father ordered the peony seed to be planted. "Let me know when it blooms," he said. Some months later, the day came; he approached the peony, and sniffed its great flower. Sonduk was right! It had no scent.

HOLY BONES AND TRUE BONES

Ancient cultures used a variety of things to predict the future. These oracles might be anything from tea leaves to the livers of animals. In Asia, bones of animals, such as deer or oxen, or antlers had long been used for this purpose. In Korea, the word "bone" had a sacred connotation. Eventually the Silla culture of Korea developed a status system, based on rank. The highest-ranking clan was divided into the "Holy Bone" and the "True Bone" ranks. Only those who were "Holy Bone" could rule.

He was intensely happy to see this proof of his daughter's wisdom. He had no son to follow him as ruler, but he had Sonduk. "She knows how to see into what she sees and hears," he said. "She'll make a great ruler of Silla when I'm gone."

And sure enough, she did. During the Three Kingdoms period of ancient Korea in which Sonduk lived, women of Silla (the kingdom that occupied the southern portion of the Korean peninsula) had a stronger position in society than elsewhere. Women of the highest rank of royalty, called the Holy Bone rank, could inherit and rule.

Sonduk may have been in her twenties (or even older) when she became queen. Then she had to look the part. She was no longer free to roam the countryside or ride her horse, wearing any old pair of trousers. In winter, she wore a full, pleated skirt of embroidered red silk—a color no one else was permitted to wear—over her trousers. She rode in a fancy chariot instead of dashing about on horseback. Her blouses had wide sleeves, trimmed with brilliant colors; her earrings were heavy objects of pure gold or silver. Sometimes Sonduk wore a wig to add to the beauty of her own long braids, twisted in a bun.

SONDUK WORE EARRINGS LIKE THESE, AND A CROWN LIKE THE ONE ON PAGE IX.

For state occasions, she carefully put on one of her lacy crowns. The crowns were up to two feet tall, and had hundreds of tiny gold shapes and tiger claws of jade suspended from tiny gold wires. As Queen Sonduk moved her head, the spangles of gold and jade danced like raindrops and sang with a special music.

Sonduk soon had many opportunities to do more than dress the part of queen. Her land of Silla had long had problems with Koguryo and Paekche, the other two kingdoms on the Korean peninsula. When she began to reign in 632, things came to a boil. The other kingdoms formed a temporary alliance and ganged up on Silla, blocking access to the Yellow Sea and isolating Sonduk's country. Queen Sonduk remembered the friendly gestures of the T'ang emperor of China over past years; he'd sent peonies and gifts. Would he help her negotiate a truce with her neighbor? Sonduk got a "yes," and soon she and the emperor had won a temporary peace, at least with Koguryo.

Meanwhile, Paekche, the other aggressor next door, secretly planned a military invasion of Silla. Now some folks bragged that Queen Sonduk had powers beyond her obvious intelligence and good judgment; it was even whispered she could predict future

CHINA'S GOLDEN AGE MADE KOREA GOLDEN, TOO

During Queen Sonduk's time, China was ruled by the T'ang Dynasty emperors. This three-hundred-year period (618–906) was called the Golden Age of China, a time when art, ceramics such as fine porcelain vases, poetry, and science flourished as never before. Both Korea and Japan were heavily influenced by their powerful big neighbor—especially when it came to the spread of Buddhism and the growth of the arts. In Sonduk's day, her Silla kingdom of Korea and China were allies; later, China tried to gobble up all three kingdoms on the Korean peninsula, but it never did conquer Silla.

Thanks to Queen Sonduk's interest in the nature of heaven and earth, astronomers and astrologers in her time got to study the skies from the Tower of the Moon and Stars. She made its construction her own pet project. The ancient stones of this 1,350-year-old observatory were assembled in a mathematically intriguing pattern. There are exactly 365 large stones used to build the tower. The base stones number 12, as do the levels of stones above and below a central window. Astronomers who worked in the tower left behind complex star charts, now on display at Kyong-ju's National Museum.

events. Clairvoyant powers would certainly help explain what happened next.

The queen, who still enjoyed studying the natural world, spotted a huge mass of frogs gathering in a field. Seeing them, she immediately went to her most trusted general and said, "The Paekche army is on its way to invade us—we've got to take action!"

She was right, of course; and as a result, her army was prepared. The Silla forces drove the Paekche army to defeat.

Not all of Sonduk's feats were mystical or military. To further her early love of astronomy, she built the first observatory in Asia. Called Ch'omsong-dae or Tower of the Moon and Stars, its graceful shape still stands in old Kyong-ju, now in South Korea. Sonduk also made sure that important Buddhist temples and pagodas got built. (One of them, a square pagoda of seven stone stories, still bears her name.)

Thanks to her diplomatic ties with the emperor of China, she initiated an educational exchange program with that country. During the sixteen years of her reign, many Korean students from Silla were sent to China for higher education; they returned home as seasoned scholars. Chajang, the most famous scholar, studied the Buddhist scriptures in China; when he returned to Silla, he made Sonduk proud by giving Korean Buddhism new life. Above the capital city, on a mountaintop called Odae-san or South Mountain, the queen asked Chajang to build another Buddhist temple among the pines. (Sangwon-sa temple is still a favorite destination for hikers and tourists.)

Although we know quite a bit about Queen Sonduk's early life and we can still admire parts of her remarkable architectural legacy, her last chapter is a question mark. Did Sonduk marry? Did she have children? Did she step down from the throne, or was she pushed? The answers aren't clear. What we do know is that Queen Sonduk ended her sixteen-year reign as she had begun it—by putting down a rebellion. In 647, her cousin Chindok succeeded her to become Silla's second queen to rule on her own.

CHAPTER 12

Komyo and Koken

(AROUND 700-770)

The famous mother and daughter duo of Komyo and Koken lived during the extraordinary Nara period in Japan, which lasted for almost one hundred years. During that time, the culture of the entire country blossomed—and Komyo and Koken did much to make it flower.

Born in 701, Komyo came from one of Japan's most powerful families—the Fujiwaras. Over the years, Komyo's clan had gotten more land than almost anyone else; they were so powerful that they won an unusual privilege: the right not to pay any taxes!

Nara was Komyo's hometown. Lovely and green, nestled in hills and forests, the little city graced the foot of Mount Mikasa. When Komyo was nine, Nara became the permanent capital of Japan. It began to grow; by the time Komyo married Emperor Shomu, more than 200,000 people lived along its gracious streets. The city of Nara was modeled after Ch'ang-an, the fabulous capital city of neighboring China.

Another import from China had swept the country—Buddhism. Nara was its religious center. Because she had married, Komyo could not become a Buddhist nun. She was, however, very much of an advocate for her religion.

When her husband Shomu became emperor in 724, she said, "My dream is to see temples and nunneries and other works of Buddha all over our land. Will you help me?"

By now, Komyo and her husband had a lively six-year-old named Koken. Other children had been born to the couple, but only Koken survived childhood. Empress Komyo moved about Nara like a hummingbird, a nonstop blur of action, taking her daughter everywhere she went.

Komyo wasn't your everyday empress, dropping in to make a speech or cut the ribbon for a grand opening. She founded places of healing and refuge where the homeless, the starving, and the ill could find free help. Often, she could be seen helping the nuns at her charitable institutions, passing out herbal remedies. Sometimes she even washed the bodies of the patients.

Koken was the light of Komyo's life. Later she became what her mother could not—a Buddhist nun. She took her vows, shaving her head and putting on saffron robes. For years, the two of them traveled around the Nara region and to other parts of Japan, intent on bringing health care and spiritual comfort to everyone who needed it.

But life wasn't all sunshine. A smallpox epidemic raged for two years, taking many lives. It hit the royal court at Nara especially hard. Then Emperor Shomu began to have severe eye problems.

"We must do more," Koken and Komyo said. In 745, they tackled a project they were sure would be pleasing to Buddha. With the emperor's help, the two women began to build a variety of temples, including Todaiji Temple, a vast complex of towers, pagodas, and shrines. The complex covered seven square blocks and took years to complete.

They put up a special temple to the Healing Buddha, called Shin-Yakushiji. Even so, Shomu's eyesight got worse. Finally, in 749, he called Komyo and Koken to his side. "One of you must take over for me," he said. Neither wanted to leave the work she was doing. But finally it was decided: daughter Koken would leave the world of the spirit, and take the throne of Japan.

Now thirty-three, Koken might not have wanted to become empress very much. But once she accepted the responsibility, she plunged in with great vigor. One of her first challenges was to complete a huge bronze statue of the Buddha for Todaiji, so that the temple complex could be consecrated. Time after time, the artisans came to her. "The casting has failed. The statue cracked," they said. "We cannot give up," Koken would say.

At long last, Todaiji Temple and its Buddha, a seventy-two-foot figure of bronze covered with a shimmering layer of pure gold

WHEN "EMPEROR" COULD MEAN "EMPRESS"

Koken was the sixth and last woman in a great tradition of female rulers in Japan during the period from the sixth to the eighth centuries. She carried the honorific title *tenno*, a word that translates as "emperor."

Other women who ruled included Suiko, the first woman to reign (between 592 and 628); Kogyoku; and Gemmei. During her reign, Gemmei became known for several firsts, including the production of both the earliest known historical work and the earliest topography of Japan. In 710, she also established the first permanent capital at Nara. Before Gemmei said "That's it—we're staying put," the capital city moved every single time that a ruler died.

(housed in a wooden building that is still the largest timber structure in the world), were ready. Empress Koken, accompanied by her mother Komyo and her nearly blind father, led the ceremony. The empress announced that she had brought five thousand Buddhist priests to attend the shrine and read the sacred books. From all over Japan, more than ten thousand worshippers gathered on the exquisite grounds. Everyone agreed it was the most splendid ceremony of the century.

When her father and mother died around 760, Koken grieved a long while. One of her main advisers suggested that the empress should step down in favor of Junnin, one of her kinsmen. "That way, you can return to the Buddhist life," he slyly said.

Her other advisers were dumbfounded. "Junnin has no right to rule," they said. But Koken did step down. After five years, however, things were so bad that she was persuaded by her personal doctor and confidant Dokyo to banish Junnin and take up empressing again.

Dokyo fought and killed Koken's other main adviser, then moved into the palace with Empress Koken. Soon she was giving him fancy titles once reserved for rulers alone.

Fortunately, Koken wasn't entirely blinded by love or loyalty. Around 768, ambitious Dokyo tried to talk her into abdicating or stepping down—this time in *his* favor! Koken said, "But you're a commoner. I need to consult an oracle about this." She hurried off to the coastal town of Uwa to consult an ancient Shinto deity called Hachiman, an oracle famous for its accuracy. The oracle had bad news for Dokyo—and he quickly disappeared from the scene.

Koken did not forget the common people. In fact, the epidemics that regularly terrorized Japan had the empress determined to find a solution. Like everyone else in eighth-century Japan, Koken believed in disease demons. In her readings, she came across something the Buddha had once suggested for lengthening life. It was a charm called a *dharani.* Buddha said, "Whoever wishes to gain power from the dharani charm must copy it seventy-seven times and place the copies in a pagoda."

Koken always made grand plans, and the dharani charm gave her a big idea: to lengthen life for every single person in Japan! She immediately ordered one million small wooden pagodas; inside of each would go a dharani charm—twenty-five lines of Japanese religious text, printed one by one with copper blocks. The printing alone must have been a major project! Once printed, the paper strips were rolled up and placed inside the pagodas. Most of the pagodas were three-storied and about five inches high. One out of 10,000 was seven-storied; and one out of 100,000 was thirteen-storied. (These were all lucky numbers.)

In 770, this big project was finished. Workers hurried to place the charms in every temple in the land.

Soon the charms faced their first test; a new smallpox epidemic hit Japan. In a sadly ironic turn of events, Empress Koken, after all her hard work, became one of its first victims.

ONE OF KOKEN'S PLAGUE-FIGHTING CHARMS, WITH ITS WOODEN PAGODA, NOW LIVES IN A MUSEUM.

BUDDHISM: REPEAT AFTER ME

Buddhism, a religion born in India in the sixth century B.C., had eight paths toward *nirvana* or enlightenment. One path was "right practice." To Buddhists, actions like donating money or becoming a nun spoke louder than words. Another way to please Buddha was to duplicate sacred writings. People made stencils. They carved images in stone and took rubbings from them, and they used block printing to make thousands of impressions. Or, in the case of Koken, millions!

Murasaki Shikibu

(ABOUT 978-1030)

THIS IS HOW
MURASAKI SHIKIBU
SIGNED HER POEMS
AND PROSE.

Murasaki Shikibu, whose name means "purple wisteria blossom," was born in the ancient capital of Kyoto, Japan. Back then, it was called Heian-kyo or "capital of peace and tranquility." Like Washington, D.C., Shikibu's city was famous for its spring flowers—above all, the cherry blossoms. Like pink and white clouds, the cherry trees floated up nearby hillsides, nearly hiding the many Buddhist temples from view. Heian-kyo was full of aristocrats and officials, nicknamed "cloud dwellers" by those not so fortunate.

Young Shikibu came from a family with little money; they, however, took comfort from their modest connections with the high and the mighty. The Murasakis could claim a distant kinship with the powerful Fujiwara clan, who dominated court politics during the Heian period, from 800 to 1100 or so. The Murasaki household was a literary place, where as a child Shikibu often heard her parents recite poetry they had composed.

In her diary, Shikibu described herself as unsociable, conceited about her looks, fond of old stories, and gentle. Judging by her life, she was also stubborn as a mule about going after her goals in life.

Born about 978, she lived in an era of peace, prosperity, elegance, and slow pace. By her day, a number of Japanese women made their marks as writers and poets. Even so, girls had a tough time getting an education—and making use of it.

Most people said, "Japanese writing is good enough for women—that is, if they're going to read and write at all."

Shikibu's brothers, however, got to study the high-prestige subjects: Chinese poetry, literature, and the beautiful and complex art of Chinese brush-writing. She was shut out; fortunately, no one stopped the young girl from hanging about during the daily lessons of her older brother.

COLLEAGUES IN CREATIVITY

There were many talented Japanese women writers in Shikibu's time. Sharp-tongued Shikibu didn't have much good to say about her fellow artists, though. For instance, about Sei Shonagon, a lady-in-waiting who wrote a racy tell-all, she said: "Sei's most marked characteristic is her extraordinary self-satisfaction. But examine the pretentious compositions in Chinese script which she scatters so liberally over the Court, and you will find them to be a mere patchwork of blunders." Famed poet Izumi Shikibu wrote a diary in which she imbedded poetry and letters. Our Shikibu, however, described her as "an amusing letter-writer, but there is something not very satisfactory about her . . . she does not seem to produce anything that one can call serious poetry."

As Shikibu later recalled, "My father was anxious to make a good Chinese scholar of my brother Nobunori, and often came to hear him read his lessons. On these occasions, I was always present, and so quick to pick up the language that I soon could prompt my brother whenever he got stuck."

Her father would sigh and say to Shikibu: "If only you were a boy, how proud and happy I should be!"

Like today, scholars in Shikibu's time sometimes got labeled as eggheads or nerds. Shikibu wrote in her diary: "It wasn't long before I repented of having distinguished myself. Person after person assured me that even boys generally become very unpopular if it's discovered that they are fond of their books. For a girl, of course, it would be even worse."

Shikibu began to keep her knowledge hidden. She put away the ink and brushes used to write the symbols for Chinese. "I was careful to conceal the fact that I could write a single Chinese char-

WOMAN'S HAND AND MEN'S LETTERS

For centuries, the Japanese used *kanji* or Chinese letters to write, even though their language didn't lend itself well to them. In the Heian period, beginning about 800, a phonetic way of writing Japanese, called *hiragana*, came into being. Although daring individuals like Murasaki also studied kanji, women were generally forbidden to learn or use "men's letters," the Chinese written language of scholars and priests. Instead, women wrote in hiragana. So many of them became outstanding writers and poets that it came to be called "woman's hand." *The Tale of Genji*, for example, was written entirely in hiragana.

acter," she confessed to her diary. "This meant I got very little practice. To this day, I am shockingly clumsy with my brush."

Sometime between her sixteenth birthday and her twentieth, Murasaki Shikibu married a distant cousin of hers, a dashing lieutenant in the Imperial Guard. Within a few years, the couple had two daughters. Quietly, stubbornly, Shikibu shared her education with them, teaching her youngsters to read, write, and appreciate poetry.

In 1001, her family life shattered like a fancy porcelain vase. Her husband died unexpectedly—possibly of the plague. It just wouldn't do for a widow of the Fujiwara clan to live independently, the family argued.

"You shall marry again, and well," her father promised. Before he could act on his promise (or threat), he was offered the job of governor for a distant province to the north of Kyoto. The family was newly worried. The chances of finding a good catch for Shikibu there were slim.

By now, however, others knew about Shikibu's keen mind and literary talents—even though she'd kept a low profile. After her husband's death, Shikibu had started writing a romantic and complex story. She called it *The World of the Shining Prince* or *The Tale of Genji*.

The Emperor of Japan himself heard about Shikibu's as yet unfinished book. He had chapters read to him, and said, "This lady must be terribly learned."

His daughter, the Empress Akiko, got very excited. "I want this woman as a teacher!" she said. At sweet sixteen, the empress was a hardcore student, a tireless learner—and a bit of a prude. No boyfriends or flirtations for her—or for the ladies of her court, either. She wouldn't let her attendants dress in stylish gowns. Behavior as well as clothes had to be dull and modest.

Soon it was all arranged; Shikibu's father agreed that his daughter would serve the Empress Akiko at the Imperial Court. (Her children evidently were cared for by servants in the parents' household.)

Now about twenty-six years old, Lady Murasaki gamely did whatever young Akiko ordered. As time went on, she looked with longing at the livelier court held by Princess Senshi, the emperor's

aunt. "The princess and her ladies are always going off to see the sunset . . . or to hear a nightingale among the flowering trees," she wrote in her trusty diary. Oh, to be one of the Senshi gang! "In her court, I'd be allowed to live buried in my own thoughts like a tree-stump in the earth," she wrote wistfully. "At the same time, they wouldn't expect me to hide from every man I hadn't yet met. And even if I made a few remarks to such a person, I shouldn't be thought lost to all shame. Indeed, I can imagine myself under such circumstances becoming, after a certain amount of practice, quite lively and amusing!"

Her social life may have been cramped. But Shikibu did have a daring—even dangerous—assignment. Young Empress Akiko had a secret passion. It didn't involve the opposite sex. It involved language. She burned to learn Chinese—the main subject forbidden to Japanese women. "Too difficult!" proclaimed the male scholars. Shikibu and the empress knew better. Eventually Akiko talked Shikibu into giving her lessons, working from books in the library of Chinese literature that Murasaki had inherited when her husband died. No one ever learned of their "mission impossible," either—until many years later, when Shikibu's diary was published.

Meanwhile, the writer continued to work on her own secret project: finishing *The Tale of Genji.* She probably had trouble figuring out where to store her manuscript; the romantic tale kept getting longer and longer. All told, the manuscript had fifty-four chapters! (In one of its English translations, the book runs more than 1,100 pages—over a million words.)

Murasaki Shikibu needed writing as a creative outlet. It was frustrating, living in the beautiful but confining fishbowl of the

Kyoto court. Shikibu had the emotional support and help of a friend, a lady-in-waiting named Saisho. She and Saisho both hated the rowdy behavior at drinking festivities they were required to attend. The friends did their best to look out for one another.

There were more serene courtly activities, too. Thanks to Shikibu's writings, we can easily picture them. For instance, the noblemen and ladies might adjourn outdoors on a crisp fall day to admire the maple trees in fiery bloom around Kyoto and to compose poems in their honor.

Or Shikibu and Saisho would take part in an afternoon incense party. Dressed in their many-layered gowns, soft and brilliant as flower petals, the guests sat while incenses of sandalwood, cedar, and other rare aromatics were burned. As Shikibu and the others "listened" to the incense, two players were named "it." They would take turns spinning a story, taking their inspiration from the fantastic images that came to mind as they sniffed the scented air. (The Japanese thought that incense brought peace,

FASHION CRAZES IN THE HEIAN WORLD

Long hair was the rage in tenth-century Japan; the most admired female tresses reached the ground. At religious ceremonies where a woman became a nun and had to cut off her hair, men and women actually wept. The fashion-conscious female of Heian times also powdered her face to a chalky white, plucked out her eyebrows, and blackened her teeth with iron and gallnut. To be in style, a woman wore a set of unlined silk robes, usually twelve of them, whose sleeves were different lengths so everyone could admire the elegant array of colors and patterns.

a sense of companionship, and purity of body and mind—with no hangovers, either.)

There are many mysteries about the author of *The Tale of Genji.* Her masterpiece, although very long, appears unfinished. It's thought that Shikibu went into a nunnery in her later years, but accounts don't agree. We don't know how her daughters grew up, or what they were like. But there is no mystery about Murasaki's talent or fame, which continues to bloom as brilliantly as the wisteria flowers still do each spring in Japan.

© British Museum. Used with permission.

CHAPTER 14

Li Ch'ing-chao

(1084-1151)

I n nine out of ten Chinese families, Li Ch'ing-chao wouldn't have been welcome. China was a country where parents traditionally longed for boy babies. The birth of another female? A disaster, most families would call it. But when Ch'ing-chao was born in 1084, her parents didn't mourn, get angry, ignore her, or expose her to die, as some would have.

Maybe the good feeling came from her mother Li Ke-fei, a creative free spirit who aspired to be a writer and wrote poetry. Female talent ran in the family; Ch'ing-chao's grandmother Wang Kung-ch'en had been a scholar. People still talked with awe about her top score in academic exams.

During Ch'ing-chao's early life, she lived in Tsinan, on the muddy banks of the Yellow River. A tranquil city famous for its silks and its one hundred springs, it was the capital of Shangtung Province.

Ch'ing-chao had a remarkably happy home, by the sound of

it. The things her parents cared about were her—and poetry. Both her parents hung out with well-known poets, like Su Tung-p'o. He was a household name in China, even though he got into hot water from time to time for his sassy verses that criticized the government. Often he would come to their home and help Ch'ing-chao's mother by critiquing her poetry. Ch'ing-chao loved to hear him recite and sing.

Ch'ing-chao didn't marry until she was seventeen—practically an old lady by Asian standards. She adored her new husband, Chao Ming-ch'eng. And he felt the same way. He was twenty-one, and still a student at the imperial university. Ch'ing-chao and Ming-ch'eng had so much in common. Both were crazy about old books, antiques, and fine art. They loved poetry and collected books of poems, which were calligraphed or brush-painted with Chinese symbols. Neither one of them cared about having fancy clothes, elaborate meals, or the million-and-one luxuries that people of their high social status insisted upon.

Ch'ing-chao later wrote about the happy-go-lucky times she and her husband enjoyed when first married: "At the beginning

THE MOST COMMON NAME ON EARTH

Even in Ch'ing-chao's time, ten centuries ago, her last name of Li was the equivalent of Smith or Jones in English. Today more people in the world bear the surname Li than any other—over 87 million people in mainland China alone!

and the middle of the month, he would pawn one of his robes for half a thousand cash, walk into the Hsiang Kuo Monastery, and buy some rubbings and books plus some fruit and nuts to bring home. The two of us would open the books, admire the rubbings, and exchange remarks of appreciation while munching the food, calling ourselves citizens of the utopian period of Ko Tien in antiquity."

Meanwhile, Ch'ing-chao was maturing into a poet of great stature. Since she'd been a child, she'd studied the masters of *tz'u* poetry. Sung to music, tz'u had become more popular than the traditional *shih* poetry that had been written for centuries. Tz'u poets sometimes set their poems to existing popular tunes. Occasionally, they composed the music, too. Over the years, Ch'ing-chao became known as the best female tz'u poet China had ever had. (It looks like she wanted to be the best tz'u poet of any gender; throughout her life, she studied—and often criticized—the tz'u poetry of other poets, working endlessly to make hers superior.)

Ch'ing-chao and her husband devised their own special nights at home. After dinner, they went to sit in the area they called "the Returned Year Room," where they lit candles and made tea. That day, Ming-ch'eng might have brought home a choice scroll or a tripod of bronze. The two of them would exclaim over their new finds, examine them for flaws, and play guessing games about their history. Sometimes they played a "Jeopardy" game they'd invented. "Here's your topic!" Ch'ing-chao would say, giving him a subject while she picked up one of their old or new books at random. Ming-ch'eng would have to guess the exact page number on which the topic would be found. The winner of the challenge got to drink tea first. Sometimes they laughed so hard, they spilled their tea all over their laps.

Ch'ing-chao and her husband loved to throw parties, too. Their poetry nights became famous among their literary friends. The whole crowd enjoyed seeing what new objects of beauty or weird curiosities the two antiquarians had discovered that week or month.

Their collections grew and grew. Even though Ming-ch'eng eventually had several government jobs, their finances were hopeless. They spent all the money they had on seals (the small objects that Chinese people used to sign their documents), paintings, rare books, calligraphy, bronzes, rubbings taken from old inscriptions, and manuscripts. Sometimes the two of them would publish a book of essays or poetry Ch'ing-chao had written, or reprint a rare out-of-print edition. If there wasn't enough money on hand, the couple would pawn something they could live without, so they could publish the new project.

For twenty-five years, they lived like this: poor in money but rich in love and cultural treasures. In 1126, their quiet happiness was shattered by dramatic events. From the north came the no-

madic Chin Tartars, a swarm of human locusts that began to gobble up China, province by province. Soon all of China seemed to be on the road, fleeing south. The imperial court of the Sung Dynasty, the emperor included, were made prisoners of war.

"We can't leave," Ch'ing-chao and Ming-ch'eng told each other. "What will become of our wonderful art—our precious books? Who will look after the fragile and rare documents we've saved from three ancient dynasties?" Both their families fled; each day, new catastrophes made life harder in the city.

In the end, they had to leave—or face destruction. It nearly killed them, deciding what could be taken, and what treasures from their art collection had to remain behind. As their world collapsed, Ch'ing-chao and Ming-ch'eng finally scurried south to a spot of temporary safety, dragging everything they possibly could with them. Then Ming-ch'eng fell ill. He never did recover from the shock and despair. In 1129, he died, leaving Ch'ing-chao a widow at the age of forty-five.

She didn't have time to mourn properly; she had to push on. Now on the brink of disaster financially, Ch'ing-chao had to sell their treasures, one by one, just to move south. At last she reached Hangchow, a city of eleven thousand bridges and numberless lakes, which had been designated the temporary capital of the Sung court.

In this calm city sanctuary, she could have relaxed. But she didn't. Chi'ng-chao set out to do the only thing she thought was a proper remembrance of her dear husband. She gladly parted with more art and books to raise money. At last she was able to publish Ming-ch'eng's manuscript on antiques, called *Records of Metals and Stones*. Then she wrote a preface for the book, a loving evocation of their life together. It was a gift that kept on giving. Most of Ch'ing-chao's own books (six books of poetry, seven of essays) got lost in the turmoil of the times—but the preface she wrote to, and about, her husband and their relationship remains to this day.

LI CH'ING-CHAO AND HER LEGACY OF LOVE

The handful of poems we still have from China's most revered female poet are wonderful. One in particular is unique: it's the only known example of a woman using the religious and philosophical path called the Tao or "the Way" in a mystical poem. Called "To the tune 'The Honor of a Fisherman,'" it uses Taoist imagery, such as the roc bird (which represented the human nervous system). But the songs of hers that move us most are the ones that speak about her husband and lost love, Chao Ming-ch'eng:

> *My heart revives with the spring.*
> *But now there is no one to share with me*
> *The joys of wine and poetry.*
> *Tears streak my rouge.*
> *My hairpins are too heavy.*
> *I put on my new quilted robe*
> *Sewn with gold thread*
> *And throw myself against a pile of pillows,*
> *Crushing my phoenix hairpins.*
> *Alone, all I can embrace is my sorrow.*
> *I know a good dream will not come.*
> *So I stay up until past midnight*
> *Trimming the lamp flower's smoking wick.*

N ote: most of the primary sources used to write these biographies are difficult to read and understand, even for adults. The books noted below are suitable for motivated younger readers; some contain primary source materials.

Ashby, Ruth, et al. *Herstory: Women Who Changed the World.* (Viking 1995). Written for young adult readers.

Bagley, J.J. *Historical Interpretation: Sources of English Medieval History, 1066-1540.* (Penguin 1965).

Barnstone, Willis. *A Book of Women Poets.* (Schocken Books/Random House 1992 rev. edition).

Bogin, Meg. *The Women Troubadours.* (Norton 1980).

Boulding, Elise. *The Underside of History.* (SAGE Publications 1992).

Brooke, Elizabeth. *Women Healers.* (Healing Arts Press 1995).

Chibnall, Marjorie. *The Empress Matilda*. (Blackwell Publishers 1991).

Comnena, Anna. *The Alexiad*. (Penguin 1969).

Forbes, Malcolm. *Women Who Made a Difference*. (Simon & Schuster 1990). Written for young adult readers.

Henry, Sondra, et al. *Written Out of History: Jewish Foremothers*. (Biblio Press 1990). Damia al-Kahina.

Hildegard of Bingen. *Illuminations*. (Bear Publishing 1985).

Kelly, S., et al. *Saints Preserve Us!* (Random House 1993). Clare.

Kim, Yung-chung, ed. *Women of Korea, A History from Ancient Times to 1945*. (Ewha Womans University Press 1976). Sonduk.

Labarge, Margaret. *Medieval Travellers*. (Norton 1982). Mahaut.

León, Vicki. *Uppity Women of Medieval Times*. (Conari Press 1997).

Magnusson, Magnus, et al. *Laxdaela Saga*. (Penguin 1969). Aud the Deep-Minded.

Meade, Marion. *Eleanor of Aquitaine*. (Penguin 1977).

Minai, Naila. *Women in Islam*. (Seaview Books 1981). Khadija.

Morris, Ivan. *The World of the Shining Prince*. (Penguin 1964). Murasaki Shikibu.

Murasaki, Shikibu. *The Tale of Genji*. (Modern Library 1960).

Ogilvie, Marilyn. *Women in Science: Antiquity Through the 19th Century*. (MIT Press 1993). Trotula.

Power, Eileen. *Medieval Women*. (Cambridge University Press 1975).

Rexroth, Kenneth, and Atsumi, Ikuko. *The Burning Heart: Women Poets of Japan.* (Seabury Press 1977).

Rexroth, Kenneth, et al. *Li Ch'ing-chao: Complete Poems.* (New Directions 1979).

Rexroth, Kenneth, et al. *The Orchid Boat: Women Poets of China.* (Seabury Press 1972).

Seidensticker, Edward, trans. *The Gossamer Years: A Diary by a Noblewoman of Heian Japan.* (Charles Tuttle 1978).

T I M E L I N E

(Most dates here and throughout the book are approximate.)

500-700

Khadija of Arabia: 555–619

Sonduk of Korea: about 610–647

Damia al-Kahina of North Africa: active around 680

700-900

Komyo and Koken of Japan: around 700–770

Aud the Deep-Minded of Norway: active around 900

900-1100

Murasaki Shikibu of Japan: about 978–1030

Trotula of Salerno, Italy: active around 1080

Anna Comnena of Constantinople: 1083–around 1148

Li Ch'ing-chao of China: 1084–1151

Hildegard of Bingen, Germany: 1098–1179

1100-1350

Matilda of England: 1102–1167

Eleanor of Aquitaine, France: about 1122–1204

Clare of Assisi, Italy: about 1193–1252

Mahaut of Artois, France: around 1275–1329